The Quest

AN EXCURSION TOWARD INTIMACY WITH GOD

BETH MOORE

LifeWay Press® Nashville, Tennessee

Published by LifeWay Press® • ©2017 Beth Moore • Reprinted September 2018

ISBN 978-1-4627-6660-4
Item 005796350
Dewey decimal classification: 248.843
Subject heading: CURIOSITY / DISCIPLESHIP / SPIRITUAL LIFE

To order additional copies of this resource, write LifeWay Church Resources Customer Service; One LifeWay Plaza; Nashville, TN 37234-0113; FAX order to 615.251.5933; call toll-free 800.458.2772; email orderentry@lifeway.com; order online at LifeWay.com; or visit the LifeWay Christian Store serving you.

Printed in the United States of America.
Adult Ministry Publishing, LifeWay Church Resources,
One LifeWay Plaza, Nashville, TN 37234-0152

Contents

6 START HERE

8 ONE

44 TWO

84 THREE

124 FOUR

166 FIVE

208 SIX

210 LEADER GUIDE

218 ENDNOTES

219 QUESTIONS FOR YOUR QUEST

Dedication

To my Living Proof Live worship team -

Nia Allen, Alexis Cruz, Kevin Jones, Lici Flowers,
Julie Goss, Tammy Jensen, Albert Kiteck,
Kevin Perry, Stephen Proctor, Seth and Nirva Ready, Wes Willett,
and, of course, your incomparable leader,
Travis Cottrell, and his bride, Angela.

Come rain or shine, come hail or high-water, in hard times and in ease,
in sickness and in health, with kidney stones and poison ivy,
laryngitis and post-nasal drip,
in fellowship halls, sanctuaries, arenas, gyms, and locker rooms,
there you've been.
Year in, year out.
Faithful. Christlike.
Hilarious.
Mischievous.
Unreasonably gifted.

Some of the most memorable miles on my quest are accrued
walking, running, singing, strumming with you.

Good grief, I love you so much.

Beth

About the Author

BETH MOORE is a best-selling book and Bible study author and a dynamic teacher whose conferences take her across the globe. Beth lives in Houston, Texas, where she leads Living Proof Ministries with the purpose of encouraging and teaching women to know and love Jesus through the study of Scripture.

Beth and her husband, Keith, have two adult daughters and three delightful grandchildren. They are devoted to the local church and have the privilege of attending Bayou City Fellowship in Houston, Texas.

Beth's life is full of activity, but one commitment remains constant: counting all things but loss for the excellence of knowing Christ Jesus, the Lord (Phil. 3:8).

Go to LifeWay.com/TheQuest for downloadable social media images to share what you're learning from this study with your friends.

The Quest STARTS HERE

Hey, Fellow Traveler!

I'm so happy to have you on this quest. I'd love to tell you a little bit about what to expect because I'm excited about it and anxious to give you a glimpse. What you're holding in your hands is not an in-depth Bible study like the ones I've had the joy of writing on the patriarchs of Genesis, for example, and on books of the Bible like Daniel, Esther, James, 1 and 2 Thessalonians, and 2 Timothy. *The Quest* is a temporary detour from my usual approach in order to focus entirely on one colossal goal: to offer an excursion packed with Scripture and set up specifically to increase an individual's intimacy with God.

You'll be invited to multiple settings in Scripture, spotlighting conversations that can readily kindle your own dialogue with God. How can we mortals dialogue with an unseen God? When He speaks to us through His Word, we can learn to speak back. This practice transforms Bible reading into what God wants most: reading that generates relationship. Even the simplest form of dialogue can make a world of difference. "Lord, this verse is confusing to me," or "Please keep me focused in my Bible reading, God," or "Jesus, open my mind to understand the Scriptures just as You did for Your first disciples" (Luke 24:45). As you practice voicing your inward response, you're continually reminded that Bible reading doesn't occur in a vacuum. You are in the actual presence of the One who inspired every word onto the sacred page. When relating with God becomes an integral part of reading His Word, boredom moves off the table and dining takes its place.

Because nothing creates dialogue like a question, the Scripture segments you'll encounter each day include or incite an inquiry of some kind. Often, after viewing the question in its context, you'll get an opportunity to consider your own answer. When the inquiry is addressed to God and it's one you have wished you could ask, you'll also get to see eye-opening evidence that He is rarely offended by earnest questions.

This quest is about you and God. My role each day will be twofold: to set the compass and to spark the query. The compass is meant to send you a direction in God's Word that stimulates dialogue through the query. I'll engage with you in the compass section, but once you get to the query I'll drop out, and it's entirely between you and your God. There's a familiar name for what you'll be doing in the query: *praying*. My deepest hope is that someone who has struggled with prayer for years will discover how captivating, satisfying, and fruit-bearing it is.

The most frequent request I've received from women of all ages over the last two years is for help in developing a prayer life that would keep them awake and engaged with Christ and effective in Him. This series is a response to that request. It will fall woefully short of a definitive word on prayer because prayer is not a discipline we can master. I deeply hope *The Quest* will, however, kindle embers into flames and take each person one step further into the realization that all the frills and thrills on earth cannot compare to time spent with Jesus. He truly is life.

To get the very most out of this series, combine this workbook with the video sessions we taped to coincide with it. I taught the introduction (Session One) and conclusion (Session Six) in a group atmosphere much like I've done in earlier studies. However, I purposely went off road for Sessions Two, Three, Four, and Five, making them much briefer and more intimate. Ideally you'll get a chance to view all six, but if you can only watch one please prioritize the introduction. I lay out the concept far more comprehensibly in that session than I can do in this written introduction, and it will give you optimum traction to begin your journey. It's also fun, and I'm not opposed to fun. I hope you're not either. It makes life a little easier.

You will never know what it means to me to walk next to you in your journey of faith for a season. I do not take this privilege lightly. Such grace of God is unfathomable to me. He used His Word to completely transform my life and rewire my mind so I never tire of trying to talk people into Bible study. I have no greater passion than to see people come to love God lavishly because they came to know and trust Him through His incomparable Word. I pray Jesus meets you on every page.

WITH ESTEEM & AFFECTION,

Beth Moore

One

Video and audio sessions available for purchase at LifeWay.com/TheQuest.

#QuestStudy

The high hopes of the excursion before us are these:

- To ________ ______ enough _____________ to invigorate a _________ _____________.
- To _________ each __________________ into ___________ _____________ _______ ________.

quest \ *'kwest* \ noun

1. A: a jury of inquest

   B: investigation

2. an act or instance of seeking:

   A: ______________, ________________

   B: a ______________________ enterprise in ________________ ________________ usually involving ____ ______________________ ______________________[1]

Distinctions that help shape the concept of quest:

1. A quest is _________ _______ ___ __________.

jour•ney *jer-nē*\\ noun

an act or instance of __________________ from ____ ________ _____ ________________: _________[2]

2. A quest carries _________ _________________ of ____________________.

3. A _________________ is no ______________ without ___________________.

Read Genesis 3:8-11, John 1:38, Matthew 8:26, and Luke 11:13.

A proposal of five ______________________ _______________:

1. ___________ ______ _______? (Genesis 3:9)

2. _____ _______ _____ _______? (Genesis 3:11)

3. ________ _____ _______ ___________? (John 1:38)

4. _____ _____ _____ _________? (Matthew 8:26)

5. _____ _______ ________? (Luke 11:13)

Read Matthew 7:7-8.

___________.

___________.

___________.

4. A _____________ on a quest is ___ _____________.

1.1

The miles ahead of you on this excursion will take the shape of curves, straight lines, gaps, and points. Were you to trace each of those shapes with your finger in order—curve, straight line, gap, point—you'd create a map with pathways carved out of question marks. In the context of this excursion, that's how you'll know you're on the right track. Your journey begins where the assumption ends that questions mean you're on the wrong track. To make this trip, you will need to be willing at times to face gaps from the teetering edge of what appear to be cliffs or, worse yet, dead ends. You'll be challenged to embrace the fact that squinting toward indefinable silhouettes in the distant horizon can still qualify as vision through the eyes of faith.

In every generation of Christians, the authority of the Scriptures gets questioned, but the paradox is that all those questions heaped in one pile would look like a molehill next to the mountain of questions within the Bible. Since neither the ancient Hebrew of the Old Testament nor the Koine Greek of the New Testament included punctuation, we don't have the luxury of dogmatism concerning the exact number of questions. Something about it escaping our certainty seems fitting, doesn't it? Scholars estimate, however, that the Bible is home to somewhere around thirty-three hundred inquiries depending upon the translation. Here's the particularly impressive part: each of them is scrupulously God-breathed (2 Tim. 3:16). Premeditated. Author J. L. Hancock took on the burly task of meticulously locating and listing every question from Genesis 1:1 to Revelation 22:21 in the King James Version tallying an astonishing sum of 3,298.[1]

The queries are multifarious. Hundreds of questions are exchanged laterally between humans, as you would expect. But you'd also find a smattering of brow-raising inquiries between humans and animals, humans and angels, humans and demons, between God and Satan, and between Jesus and demons. The road ahead will wind around a handful of those, but the ones that will most profoundly shape our landscape will be vertical: questions man asks of God and those God asks of man. The number of those kinds of questions is staggering and beyond the mileage of this six-week excursion. However, I pray and believe the ones on this map will be enough to drive a willing traveler to behold the divine quest.

One monumental difference between traveling on foot and riding on wheels is how much you can pack. The miles ahead of us will accrue on the soles of our feet, so a wise traveler will lighten the load from the start. Do yourself a huge favor by throwing off the hindrance of overfamiliarity. If you've been in enough Christian circles, studies, services, and events to accumulate it, shed it like a snakeskin, or it will insulate you from feeling the elements. The elements are crucial to this trip. You don't want a windshield on a walk with God unless it's God Himself. You need to be able to brook the heat and the icy cold, or the prospect of extreme elements will continue to intimidate you. Nobody savors a spring breeze like the one with a face chapped by winter winds. Developing overfamiliarity with Christian terms and practices isn't hard to do, but a vital distinction must here be drawn: It's impossible to become overfamiliar with God. Mastering God is an oxymoron at its highest for "His greatness no one can fathom" (Ps. 145:3, NIV). Forsake the stale rut of tidy definitions and get out there where the dust flies.

It's impossible to become *overfamiliar* with God.

The metaphors of walking and running in reference to a mortal's relationship with God are consistently brush-stroked on pages of both testaments. Fascinatingly, the human isn't the only one doing the walking in the metaphor. Glance at each of the following verses and record who is described as walking and, if specified, where or with whom.

Genesis 3:8 ______________________________

Genesis 5:22-24 ______________________________

Genesis 6:9 ______________________________

Leviticus 26:12 ______________________________

2 Corinthians 6:16 ______________________________

____

It's a walk we're on here. So imagine being on an extended backpacking trip with someone where ground rules were set for complete freedom of conversation as long as no one asked any questions. Talk your tongues dry but no inquiries allowed. Not even a basic, "How are you feeling?," or "You getting hungry?" An interchange of statements would go well enough for a while, but, sooner or later, you'd no longer be talking with one another. You'd simply be listening to one another. That's not dialogue. That's diatribe. After enough diatribe, even the best listeners stop listening.

Unless routine has lulled us into sleepwalking, to walk with God is to be on a quest. And a quest is no quest without questions. The component of mutual inquiry is nowhere more fascinating than in a relationship with God. For starters, He doesn't answer us aloud or write across the sky like we wish He would when we ask Him a question. He has, however, written across the scroll more answers than we can absorb in a lifetime.

Turn the tables on the conversation for a moment and consider the peculiarity of God in the role of inquirer. Document specifics about God's knowledge based on these verses:

Psalm 33:13-15 ______________________________

Psalm 147:4 ______________________________

Matthew 10:29-30 ______________________________

1 John 3:20 ______________________________

____

Why man would have questions for God is obvious. We want to know what we don't know. We want things explained that aren't. But why does God ask questions of man when He already knows the answers? List every reason you can imagine.

In the opening video session, we established five divine questions that, dare we answer, have the potential to recalibrate and reignite a walk with God that has gotten off track, stuck in a cul-de-sac, or has lost steam or our interest. Start today memorizing these questions. Get them so far down in the quick of your brain that you could list them in your dreams. The first two are asked by God the Father, and the last three are asked by Jesus the Son. Some are abbreviated for easy memorization.

"WHERE are you?" (Genesis 3:9)

"WHO told you that?" (Genesis 3:11)

"WHAT are you seeking?" (John 1:38)

"WHY are you afraid?" (Matthew 8:26)

"HOW much more ... ?" (Luke 11:13)*

Circle each word that appears in all caps. Though you will encounter numerous other inquiries on the road ahead, answering these five will establish a baseline you can look back on for reflection and evaluation at the end of this trek.

Your first five days will be preoccupied with these five questions. Here's the thing. The effects of this excursion will not exceed your honesty. They will go exactly as deep as you are true. Nothing is off limits in the next six weeks except dishonesty. It will break the ankles of your walk with God.

God already knows your heart anyway. He can already read your thoughts. And when you're finished with the study, you can shred this journal if you want or burn it into ashes, but between now and then, it's the real you with the real Master of the universe. You see, what I'm proposing is this: There's something you want more than answers. You want revelation. You were made for it. So was I. Remember when I asked you earlier why on earth God would ask man questions when He already knows the answers? Perhaps He will one day offer dozens of explanations, but over and over Scripture suggests this: God, our Maker, Savior, Redeemer, and King, wants interaction with His prized creation even in all our flaws and frailties and doubts and failures. And not just interaction. He wants engagement. And not just engagement. He wants intimacy.

With *you*. Not who you wish you were or act like you are in front of spectators. *You*.

**CSB, KJV, NASB, and The Message conclude Luke 11:13 with a question mark, while ESV, NIV, and NKJV use an exclamation mark for emphasis.*

You have now officially arrived at your first query. Each day's query is between you and God alone. The query is meant to be a catalyst for dialogue. God will speak through His Word. And you, if you're willing, will speak back. Everything you write in this section will either be His words to man or your words directly to Him.

Read Genesis 1:26–2:17 and 3:1-9, noting—perhaps marking—each verse containing words God spoke directly to Adam. What question did God ask in Genesis 3:9? Record it here in bold letters.

Now, switch places with Adam and let the divine inquisition land on you. Where are you? You have somewhere to go over these next six weeks, but any accurate route to your destination begins with your present location. Write directly to God, describing where you presently are in your life. If you're in a relatively good place, tell Him about it. Get specific like you would with someone who really cares and would rejoice with you. On the other hand, you may be in a monotonous place or a desperate, momentous, miserable, painful, or lonely place. Describe where you are with complete freedom of speech to God. In all likelihood, you're in a more nuanced place than one adjective can describe. Tell Him the complexities.

Truth be told, maybe you wish you could ask God the same question: "Lord, where are You? Where have You been recently?" or "Where were You when … ?" Perhaps you know the answer biblically and theologically. Your head knows the Scripture promises that He will never leave you nor forsake you, but your heart presently feels like He is nowhere to be found. You really can ask Him where He is or, if it pertains to a previous season, where He was. Read Jeremiah 2:1-13, and then Job 23:1-10. One scenario depicts distance from God caused by man's idolatry. In the other, man was utterly innocent of blame. Let either or both of these prompt this section of your journaling to God.

Conclude your journaling today with Psalm 139:7-10, either borrowing the exact words of the psalmist or penning his expressions in your own words.

1.2

Among the six investigative questions, one stands in complete distinction from the rest, upright on the page and usually on two feet. Only one assumes an answer with a pulse. One alone obliges personage and, in the strictest sense of the word, *personality*. One alone is an intentional hand-off to an answer with opposable thumbs. Few other questions get more of our undivided attention, adoration, ire, and fascination than those that begin with the word *who*.

Leave the question *who?* out of the equation and you may still have a quest of some sort, but it's a companionless hike on a desert island at the furthest pole from intimacy with God. It's like going it alone with a canteen of saltwater when we've been offered the company of One who can turn water into wine. Intimacy is cast in complete dependency and remarkable transparency on the question *who?* In the divine quest, intimacy is most often born in what seems from a human perspective so subtle a shift that it's rarely memorable. Somewhere along the way those coming to know God veer in their inquiry from, "Who is the Lord?" to "Who are You, Lord?" That which was sought about Him begins to be sought from Him. In spiritual terms the shift is tectonic and sufficient to rattle the gates of hell.

Authentic intimacy requires the quest for both identities. In terms of intimacy with God, the oceanic question "Who are You, Lord?" writes another in the wet sand of its high tide: "Who am I, Lord?" To hold to the mentality that the second question has no place at all can be noble in its humble intent, but it is not biblical. God expended wells of ink on the parchments of Scripture to answer a question that, while it may be a distant second, it is second nonetheless. That He often uses the second question—who am I?—to bring people to the first—who is God?—is a testimony to His sheer mercy and patience. In that self-centric order, however, the question of who we are must be wholly reconsidered once we begin grasping truth about who He is. Who we believe God to be does not change Him one whit, but our identities and destinies hinge all their hopes upon it. The little we believe He can do does not make Him one ounce less able, but it makes us woefully incompetent.

These two questions—who are You, Lord? and who am I?—are imperative in the divine quest toward intimacy with God. But they are by no means the only *who?* inquiries weaving their way into our walk. *Who are others? Who is my neighbor? My friend? My authority? Who are my fellow sojourners?* And, crucially, *who is my enemy?* Identity questions reveal undistorted answers beneath the towering limelight of the Bible's overarching Q&A: Who is like the Lord? Nobody.

These two questions—who are You, Lord? and who am I?—are imperative in the *divine quest* toward intimacy with God.

Take a good look at Deuteronomy 33. What does the chapter contain?

Our heritage of faith treasured up in the Old Testament is a bank account of riches impossible to overdraw in a lifetime of study. We have the privilege of living on the completed side of the redemptive work of Jesus, the Lamb of God, foreshadowed by every Old Testament sacrifice. When we place our faith in Jesus, we go under the new covenant rather than the old covenant of ancient Israel. The church, the collective body of Jesus followers, is not synonymous with Old Testament Israel, but we share certain eloquent commonalities as the people of God. Blessings, for instance. While Deuteronomy 33 showcases twelve tribes of Israel with separate pieces of the prophetic pie, by Christ's grace we inherit "every spiritual blessing in the heavens" (Eph. 1:3).

With potential similarities in mind, read the prologue and epilogue in Deuteronomy 33:1-5,26-29, bookending the blessings of the twelve tribes. (Jeshurun is a poetic name for Israel meaning "upright" or "straight."[2])

Perhaps no concept is more familiar to us than the one expressed in the first few words of Deuteronomy 33:3. However, there's also no concept more beautiful or transforming to those who believe it. Write the first portion of Deuteronomy 33:3.

What imagery does Deuteronomy 33:26-27 paint of the otherness of God?

Compare Deuteronomy 33:26 and 33:29. What stunning common characteristic is intimated?

Let this sink in from the surface of your belief system down to the roots: because there is no one like our God, there is no one like His people. This is true under both covenants. The Old Testament Israelites were naturally born into the family of God while we are reborn into it by the Spirit (John 1:11-13; 3:3). Neither birthright was about superiority. Both were about salvation. Both were dependent on grace.

Note the concept in Deuteronomy 33:29. "How happy you are, Israel! Who is like you, a people ________________________?"

In her fascinating book *Grit: the Power of Passion and Perseverance*, author and psychologist Angela Duckworth shares her findings from years of research on the secrets of outstanding achievement.

> "Identity influences every aspect of our character, but it has special relevance to grit. Often, the critical gritty-or-not decisions we make—to get up one more time; to stick it out through this miserable, exhausting summer; to run five miles with our teammates when on our own we might only run three—are a matter of identity more than anything else. Often, our passion and perseverance do not spring from a cold, calculating analysis of the costs and benefits of alternatives. Rather, the source of our strength is the person we know ourselves to be."
>
> ANGELA DUCKWORTH[3]

For people of faith, our source of strength is far more impressive. It's who we know God to be. However, if we never connect His identity with ours, the pipeline built by the cross connecting us to divine power stays mostly clogged by unbelief.

OK, now let's take a different turn with the question *who?* Throughout this opening week, you are familiarizing yourself with five recalibrating questions which I've proposed, if earnestly answered, have the capability to land you back on track in your journey with God no matter what got you off course or put you on pause. Your query on Day One circled around the first question.

Record it here.

Record the four words to the second question.

You are staring in the face of one of the most powerful and provocative questions ever posed to a mortal.

Go back to its original context and read Genesis 3:1-13. Trace the answer to the question "Who told you that?" to find the question's original source. Who told them something deceptive that led to sin?

Who you increasingly believe God to be and, in His light, believe yourself to be is not only fundamental to intimacy, it is fundamental to victory. Reread Deuteronomy 33:29 and you'll see the cords of victory and identity firmly tied together. Only because of the shield and sword of their God would they tread upon the backs of their enemies.

The similarities for New Testament believers in Ephesians 6:10-17 are gorgeous. Tie them together here:

Every defeat of a child of God in battle can be accounted to one of two causes: 1) what we have not yet learned or 2) how we have been deceived. Our victories and defeats are driven by our beliefs. So is the depth of our intimacy with God. Every time we choose sin, we are acting on a lie that usually goes like this: The world is a giver and God is a taker. The Bible is our sure footing for what is true about God, about ourselves, our pasts, our futures, about others, about our enemies, about this world and the next. To walk in truth as a child of God and be able to spot a well-spun lie buffed to a shine by the serpent, start quizzing your beliefs with this test: *Who told you that?* God equipped the body of Christ with pastors, shepherds, and teachers. They are gifts to us and we're meant to flourish under their instruction. However, they are dependable to the degree that what they say lines up with what God says. A sample interview to clarify the point:

Who are you now that you've come to Christ? I'm a new creation.

Who told you that? My pastor.

Who told him that? God, I think.

Excellent. Where did God tell him that? 2 Corinthians 5:17.

We obviously don't learn our identities from pastors and teachers alone. Our identities are also shaped by parents, siblings, peers, coaches, law enforcement, schools, experiences, environments, and fears. Another sample interview:

Tell me a few things about yourself. Well, I'm stupid. I have the worst luck. I'm fat. Sloppy. I'm terrible with money. Homely. I'm unlovable. Plain. I don't have any common sense. I'm a failure.

Who told you that? My mom.

Or was it your ex? Your classmates? Your lay-off? Your loss? Your illness? Your own self-talk?

To walk in truth with healthy bones, every "Who told you that?" needs tracing back to God in Scripture, and, if it's incongruent, it needs tossing. Adam and Eve fell for a lie and lassoed humanity back to dust with them. Their defeat was swift and severe and all for the sake of a false identity. Deception is always a thief.

This brings you to your query. All dialogue now shifts to you and God.

Each verse below expresses at least one dimension of God's complete otherness. In the space provided, profess to God what sets Him apart.

Exodus 15:11

Deuteronomy 3:24

1 Kings 8:23

Psalm 89:6-8

Isaiah 45:18

Isaiah 45:21

Maybe you've studied Scripture enough to know who you really are and what that means. But it may be that what abides on the surface of the page differs from what broods deep down within you—shaping and forming your perceptions, perspectives, and attitudes and propelling your decisions, actions, and relationships. No shame. Truth liberates. Dig past the talk way down into the depths of your core beliefs.

What do you truly believe about yourself? In the left-hand column express to God five beliefs that most impact your quality of life whether negatively or positively.

Offer an answer to God as accurately as you can for each item. May God use this twenty-five-day quest to replace any lie in those core beliefs with the truth.

GOD, I EARNESTLY SEEM TO BELIEVE THAT...	WHO TOLD YOU THAT?
1.	
2.	
3.	
4.	
5.	

Conclude by completing this sentence.

LORD, NOBODY BUT YOU ...

1.3

When I was a child swaddled in a church pew by the squirming bodies of my siblings, I'd lean forward during the hymns to spy on my grandmother and her friends. Their whole culture fascinated me. They had a certain formality about them, all widows, referring to one another as Mrs. So-and-So. Casual didn't come easy wearing pillbox hats and nylon stockings. But it was the way my grandmother cried during the singing that caught my maiden eyes. Having taken half the first stanza just to stand to their worn feet, they all held their hymnals wide open without giving them a single glance. Didn't need to. They knew the words by heart and lived the words by faith. *What a friend we have in Jesus, all our sins and griefs to bear.*[4]

My grandmother's voice quavered as tears rolled down her cheeks, making their way in a wrinkled wilderness of pink rouge. Of course, I know now why she cried during the hymns, because I'm often her these days, all the way to my aging hands. The same phenomenon happens to me during worship at church when we do congregational Scripture reading from the screens. I often choke back tears because these confessions—both sung and read—become as dear to us over the tests of time as the air in our lungs.

The power of Scripture. The life in it. The breath of it. The mystery of it. Utterable words on human tongues proclaiming the Immortal Invisible whose voice is described at times like thunder. Pray with me as we open the Scriptures today that He will give each of us eyes to increasingly behold His brilliance and beauty and give us hearts and minds to love and crave His words more than our next meal. These are holy things. Supernatural things that come not by practice alone but by crying out for them in prayer.

John 1:35-51 sketches the first scenes and inscribes the first words of Jesus found in John's Gospel. If your translation has a caption before the section beginning with verse 35, write it here.

List each question found in verses 35-51, noting who asked (inquirer), what was asked (inquiry), and to whom the question was directed (addressee).

INQUIRER	INQUIRY	ADDRESSEE

Let all that squiggly punctuation pave a road to our thematic point: questions can have a hearty place in dialogues between God and man. Matthew 7:7-8 becomes a bulldozer in the thick, thorny brush in this twenty-five-day quest. According to Christ, receiving most often comes to the ones asking and finding most often comes to the ones seeking.

Glance back at John 1:45 where you'll find the word *found* (or a form of the word) used twice. Record how it is used.

What similar statements are made in verses 39 and 46?

The disciples responded to Christ's "What are you seeking?" (ESV) with "Where are you staying?" We can't say for certain why they responded this way, but give it some thought and offer your supposition.

I find it so delightful, it's almost hard to take sitting down.

The NIV translates Jesus' question in verse 38 point-blank. "What do you want?" We don't know the inflection Jesus used in this question, but if He emphasized "you," it didn't likely carry the disparagement we often assign to it. After all, He wanted them to follow Him and later in the same Gospel would tell them they had not chosen Him, rather He had chosen them (John 15:16).

When was the last time someone besides a waiter or barista asked you what you wanted? Sometimes an answer to the question of what we desire is on the tip of our tongues. Other times, for the life of us, we can't seem to spit it out. Maybe we don't know what we really want. Perhaps at twenty we thought we did, but life came along and pummeled it to dust. On the other hand, sometimes we're caught off guard by the question or too intimidated by who's asking it for our immediate response to be our truest answer.

For those two disciples scuffling through the mud on Jordan's banks, no truer answer existed in so few words. In that one return question—Where are you staying?—they summed up a hundred answers. Here's a few:

What we want is to go with You. To be with You. To learn from You. Our teacher told us no one is like You and that You are the One we've been waiting for. The One he prepared us for. Wherever You're going is where we want to be. So, You ask us, "What are we seeking?" Rabbi, we are seeking You. What we want is YOU.

But here's the thing. It may be that we wish Jesus was our supreme desire, but, truth be told, sometimes He's not. And, if this quest is about anything at all, it's that truth be told. When God's immutable, unflappable truth is invited to invade our truthful estate, somebody notify the prison warden there's about to be a breakout.

Glance back at Christ's words to Nathanael in John 1:47. What did He say about him?

The ultimate wordsmith crafted a play on words. The patriarch Jacob's name meant *cheater, schemer, supplanter*, each of which requires a liar, and he more than qualified. God later changed Jacob's name to Israel, but more on that later in our quest. One commentator offered a more obvious wordplay of Christ's greeting to Nathanael: "an Israelite in whom there is no Jacob!"[5]

Our inner Jacob's got to go if we want to get where Jesus longs to lead us. We've viewed two of our five recalibrating questions: 1) Where are you? and 2) Who told you that? Our third question is the one Jesus asked in John 1:38: "What are you seeking?" He's unimpressed when we respond to Him with what we think He wants to hear. Imagine His play on words in sad reversal, "A Jacob in whom there is no Israel!" In other words, a schemer in whom there is no honest wrestling. Jesus is perfectly capable of handling our honesty. He knows when the real answer to the question, "What are you looking for?" is "trouble." Or money. Or security. Or sex. Or substance. Or human flesh and blood to fill a grand canyon of emptiness. Sometimes the most powerful testimony can be, "I was looking for ____________________ and found Jesus."

The Samaritan woman in John 4 didn't come to the well wanting Jesus. She came wanting water, so He introduced her to living water. She wasn't rejected for wanting the wrong thing. Jesus used what she sought to bring her to what He knew deep down in her heart she thirsted for most: a Savior who could stop the madness, forgive her sins, and give her dignity. The Messiah who knew the real version of her story and wouldn't buy her savvy diversions.

You will know the truth, and the truth will set you free. So if the Son sets you free, you really will be free.

JOHN 8:32,36

Likewise, Jesus was the last thing Saul thought he wanted when he ran into Him on the road to Damascus. He wasn't hunting for Jesus. He was hunting down Jesus' followers. You see, askers receive even if what they receive differs from what they asked. Seekers find even if what they find differs from what they sought. Doors open to the ones knocking even if an unexpected host turns the knob. At first blush, Jesus may sound like a Jacob: a supplanter who baits and switches. In reality, He sees beneath our temporal desires and foresees what we will have wanted most when we step across that finish line. Isaiah 46:10 captures a concept of titanic proportions in our quest: God knows the end from the beginning. Those seven words are game-changers in this Olympic race. They put trust in the breast of the quester.

I declare the end from the beginning, and from long ago what is not yet done, saying: my plan will take place, and I will do all my will.

ISAIAH 46:10

God knows the underlying questions driving our quests. He formed the human soul to be more compelled by desire than need except in matters of survival. Need will only carry you until the pressure is off. It's want that will keep you running come rain or shine, sleet or snow. It's want that keeps your heart in the race. When God does not give you the desire of your heart, give it time and trust and see if He ends up giving you something deeper: the heart of your desire. You may plead to have children, for example, and God may answer your prayers exactly the way you pictured. Then again, you may realize somewhere down the road that He gave you hundreds of sons and daughters in the faith as you poured out your heart for years in student ministries. He also knows when we've given up on desire altogether and we're trying to make a life out of nothing more than doing the right thing. Nothing makes you feel deader than the death of desire. If yours is dead, you're on the cusp of a resurrection and some holy desires that can thrill you without killing you and can delight you without derailing you.

What desires stir deepest within you? What are your longings? Which of those have gone enduringly unfilled? Write to God and tell Him all you long for. What you crave. Tell Him what desires drive you. You may soon realize that God planted some of those desires in your heart with His own hands.

Tell God what you keep seeking in people. Thank Him if you've found some of what you were looking for. And, then, by wildly courageous faith, thank Him for the times you haven't.

Offer Jesus the space everybody else has left empty.

Now have the courage to ask Him to exhibit His preeminence in the full spaces. In your own words, request Christ's merciful, healthy presence to be Lord in your highly esteemed relationships so that no one becomes a false Christ to you. This is protection for both you and each person in whom you've found what you were looking for. Be thankful for them but don't be intoxicated by them. Every false Christ fails.

Now, it's your turn to ask God what He wants from you and for you in any wording you wish and in any situation most pertinent. This may seem like an exercise in futility since His voice won't likely thunder from heaven. But a crucial part of the quest is discovering the power, freedom, and stirred-up affection of getting to ask. You also stand to be amazed if He chooses to reveal some of those answers in coming days.

While Jesus has individual things He wants from and for you, you can eavesdrop on the wants He presented to His Father in John 17:24-26 regarding all who belong to Him.

Write those three verses in this space but personalize Christ's intercession by replacing "they" and "them" with your first name.

Read the words of Psalm 38:9 aloud to Jesus as you conclude. Meditate on them. Memorize them. Let this truth be a tent you can rest in as you continue your journey.

Lord, my every desire is known to You;
my sighing is not hidden from You.

PSALM 38:9, HCSB

1.4

The mysteries of the incarnation are vast enough to tie the tongues of teachers, bleach the ink of writers, and dry the paints of artists. To describe it beyond the language supplied by Scripture is to automatically agree to elementary terms. How, after all, does God become man? How does a Creator adapt to hammer and nails? How does the Self-Existent adjust to hunger and thirst? How does the Knower of hearts keep company with native liars? How does the infinite squeeze into finite flesh when we who have given birth can't squeeze into our old jeans? "For the entire fullness of God's nature dwells bodily in Christ" (Col. 2:9). How does He who neither sleeps nor slumbers deal with drowsiness?

The answer: with a nap. Lest we over-identify, the same winds that rocked the boat until the bow nearly broke rocked their Creator to sleep like they were chiming "Lullaby Baby."

Read Matthew 8:23-27.

If your imagination is not wet-faced with lake water, if it is not weak-kneed, white-knuckled, or seasick, you may need to go back and read the segment again. Knowing a story turns out well can have a terrible way of taming it.

Knowing a *story* turns out well can have a terrible way of *taming* it.

"Suddenly, a violent storm arose on the sea," the 24th verse says, *"so that the boat was being swamped by the waves."*

Violent storm. The kind that can kill you. The kind that can bring professional sailors to the end of their ropes and capsize a virile man's boat like it's a little boy's toy. Wind so loud you can hardly hear what the person inches from you is yelling. Waves crashing over the side, making a pool of the hull. The boat tilts severely to the left. Your feet come out from under you. Your shoulder slams into the stern. You make your way to your knees, but your drenched clothes weigh you down like lead. Another wave. The wind punches the sails like the enormous fists of mythical gods, tossing you into your shipmates like a cosmic game of pick-up sticks.

And Jesus is sound asleep.

Matthew's choice of language interprets the storm as "an earthquake ... in the sea."[6] Somehow we never think to expect the earth to quake in the sea. Note the full momentary rebellion of three terrestrial layers: earth, sea, and wind.

"Lord, save us! We're going to die!" One day they'd realize death has no power to un-save the saved, but it was not this day.

He *asked* the question *then* calmed the sea.

Notice the peculiar order. Jesus didn't calm the sea first then ask the question. He asked the question then calmed the sea. The most baffling juxtaposition of their postures may be that He didn't bother to get up to ask the question. He asked it, then He got up and rebuked the winds and the sea.

His question to the disciples is our fourth recalibrating inquiry. Record it here in the short form we established on Day One.

Part of changing our view of the landscape on the faith-quest is dealing with fears that threaten to paralyze us or roll us up on the roadside in the fetal position. Our fears may differ, but it's likely no one is afraid of nothing. We can even be afraid of being afraid. How scared we anticipate being can keep us from ever doing. However, in some strange ways fear's relentlessness can backfire. The realization that fear, if accommodated, would know no bounds can either push us down or push us into pushing back like a small kid punching a big bully in the gut. I know this subject intimately because nothing in my life has harassed me like fear. Had I let fear have what it wanted, I'd be curled up in a far corner behind a barricaded door. So, in many ways, by the power and call of God, I pushed back. I've come close to making a life out of doing what I'm scared of.

God's words to Cain in Genesis 4:7b have a familiar ring: "Sin is crouching at the door. Its desire is for you, but you must rule over it." Fear crouched at my door. Sin did, too, of course, but perhaps our first step to freedom is becoming cognizant of copious sins that stem from our fears. Fear's desire was for me. The word *welcome* on my doormat began to take on a question mark. What would I welcome in? What would I refuse? Fear crouches, ready to pounce. Will we let it eat us alive?

For God did not give us a spirit of fear.

Our fears often change as we grow up, but we're still afraid of the dark. Of the unknown. Of what lurks in the shadows. We're afraid of going to bed alone or sometimes afraid of who's crawling in bed with us. We're afraid we won't sleep or afraid we will with nightmares that seem real. We're afraid of realizing we're not asleep at all and what we hoped was a nightmare is real.

Fear is the consummate robber. One technical distinction between a thief and a robber is that a thief works by stealth and a robber works by threat. A pickpocket, for example, is a thief. At the time of the crime the victim is oblivious. A robber, on the other hand, confronts and threatens. He wields a weapon, be it literal or psychological. Sometimes the robber follows through on the threat. Other times he doesn't. But what he's banking on is the success of the threat. Likewise, fear. We keep thinking that what we're afraid of is all there is at stake. Meanwhile, fear is robbing us blind of our joy and drenching the fire of our callings.

Write 2 Timothy 1:6-7 in this space.

Fear is also a glutton. If we let it eat away at us, it will consume us entirely before it ever gets full. Trying to eliminate all our reasons for fear is an exhausting waste of energy. On the other hand, filling up the space it's vying for is sweet revenge.

Read the following passages and write your own summations of the relationship between fear and faith (also called belief).

Isaiah 7:4-9 __________

Mark 4:40 __________

Mark 5:36 __________

Biblically speaking, fear and faith fight for the same space. Each is territorial. To illustrate the concept through metaphor, think in terms of your soul being a house and Fear and Faith are knocking at your door. Each desires to occupy expansive square footage in the house of your soul. How about some gloriously good news to those of us who have given much ground to fear? Any square foot or inch where Fear abides in your life is the precise ground Faith exists to occupy.

Fear and Faith cannot be roommates. They will not coexist. The one assigned authority automatically elbows the other off the space. Fear can't stand on a carpet of faith.

Shift the same concept from a house metaphor to that of a field. The same soil that has been fertile for fear is fertile for faith. If you can find your fear, you can always know where to send your faith. No, faith is not as easy to come by as fear, but it is colossally easier to live with. What faith costs you in tenacity, fear up-charges you in misery. Write a question mark at the end of the *welcome* on your doormat then decide what gets to come into your house.

As a follower of Christ, allow His question to His disciples in Matthew 8:26 to echo in your chest. "Why are you afraid?" Tell Him until the well of those fears—at least for now—runs dry.

With your own pen, ask Jesus to take every square inch where fear resides and replace it with faith.

God's most frequent exhortation to His people in Scripture is, by no coincidence, "do not be afraid." His wording may differ from verse to verse and translation to translation, but the urging to fearlessness is brilliantly consistent. The sheer frequency—clocking in at well over 350 times—conveys not only His gracious reassurance and bold insistence but also the divine affirmation that this terrestrial soil is fertile ground for fear. Translation: you don't have to imagine things to think this world is scary. It is scary. And being a follower of Jesus in a world increasingly hostile to the gospel is also scary. In each verse below, God bids His follower to give no place to fear, but His reasons differ gorgeously in each selection. In the space provided, record His exact explanation why not to fear. Take them personally.

Joshua 1:9

Isaiah 41:10,13

Isaiah 43:1

Isaiah 44:8

Isaiah 54:4

Luke 12:32

John 14:27

To conclude, please write Psalm 23:4 as a confession of faith.

1.5

You will land today on the fifth recalibrating question. Many other inquiries lay in wait for you on this twenty-five-day pilgrimage, but these five unroll a wide scroll for journaling your starting point. Where? Who? What? Why? How? The inquirer in each question is God Himself, the only One in existence who knows all of the answers before He asks. Don't lose sight of the majesty of this mystery for a single moment. The Creator is the Searcher—the initiating Seeker—who does not seek in order to learn. Omniscience leaves no gaps to fill or caves to mine. The lens of our telescopic understanding is tantamount to looking at the Milky Way through a straw. However, this truth shines star-like in the vastness: God seeks, at least in part, for the pure pleasure of knowing those by whom He longs to be known. Simply put, the Revelator loves revelation.

Read Luke 11:5-13. How would you state the theme of this segment?

Do Christ's bold assurances in these verses stir up any questions in you? Ask them here. Freely express any confusion.

The HCSB makes the present verb tenses in the Greek obvious: "So I say to you, keep asking, and it will be given to you. Keep searching, and you will find. Keep knocking, and the door will be opened to you" (v. 9).

Why all the emphasis on the keeping, do you think?

We're beating on these three drums—asking, searching, knocking—because they invite participants into the parade of faith instead of fostering distracted spectators who stick to the sidewalk with gum on our shoes. The action verbs set an animated rhythm to our pilgrimage songs because they train us to expect something ahead. What our Maker knows, our mouths may find hard to admit: The human soul was fashioned to prize discovery above luxury.

Anyway, spirited pilgrimage songs are the best kind. It's hard to keep your heartbeat up in a dirge. Don't misunderstand. Lament has a crucial place on the journey, and you'll find the practice in these pages. But if the playlist over your life becomes an endless lament, your gaze will fix on your feet and evaporate your vision.

Look back at Luke 11. Verses 11, 12, and 13 each includes a pair of contrasts. List them here:

v. 11 ______

v. 12 ______

v. 13 ______

Fish and snakes are both cold and slick, but one is food and the other has fangs. A scorpion can roll itself into a ball, but it is a woefully far cry from an egg. What father worth his title would put a biting snake or stinging scorpion in the palm of his child? He loves his child and treats his child well, tenderhearted to his wants, impassioned to her pleas. An affectionate father longs to say yes. The absurdity that an infinitely gracious God would do less is illustrated almost cartoonishly through the evil parent who gives good gifts.

Our fifth recalibrating question is tucked right in the middle of verse 13. Write all five questions here and, when you come to the fifth, pen it in all capital letters. We've abbreviated it to three words.

1. ______

2. ______

3. ______

4. ______

5. ______

In the first four questions, God holds the lantern for the mortal to search himself in relationship to God: Where are ______? Who told __________ that? What are __________ seeking? Why are _______ afraid? In radiant contrast, the question *how much more* will always take the gaze of the truth finder out of the murky deep of self-focus to the horizon where the sunrise spray-paints the sky.

If you then, who are evil, know how to give good gifts to your children, how much more will the heavenly Father give ... ?

LUKE 11:13a

Christ gives away the answer through the rhetoric of the question:

How much more?

So much more.

That three-word question and answer always unleashes an overflow of hope. It will never be the herald of bad news.

A comparison between Luke's wording and Matthew's wording in this slice of Christ's teaching is fascinating. Read Matthew 7:7-11. You'll see an additional contrasting pair in Matthew 7:9. List it here:

Record the difference between Matthew 7:11 and Luke 11:13.

What do you make of that?

According to early church fathers Jerome (circa AD 400) and Eusebius (circa AD 300), Luke was from Antioch.[7] A long-time traveling companion to the apostle Paul, Luke is assumed to have been a Gentile, probably Greek, since Paul did not list him among those "of the circumcision" who were his fellow workers (Col. 4:10-11). That Luke was a physician is particularly striking (Col. 4:14). The timing of his arrival in Paul's missionary journey may well suggest he originally joined him to provide medical assistance. The third Gospel was not Luke's only contribution to the canon. He also wrote the Book of Acts.

Peruse Acts 1:1–2:18, and count the number of times Luke mentioned the Holy Spirit.

By the closing words of the Book of Acts, Luke had referenced the Holy Spirit more than fifty-five times. How does Acts 10:45 hold particular significance?

After all Luke had seen, heard, and experienced, no wonder under the inspiration of God his Gospel reads, "how much more will the heavenly Father give the Holy Spirit to those who ask him?" (Luke 11:13). He knew with every scrap of his being that there was no gift on earth like the Holy Spirit. Imagine a doctor who'd built a career from systematized knowledge of scientific methods standing back and watching the Holy Spirit defy explanation and laws of nature. Luke was no gullible fool. He was adept at testing effects to determine causes. He'd seen innumerable manifestations of the Spirit through word, healing, and deed and had been employed by God to inscribe permanent records of miraculous encounters and escapades brought on by the selfsame Spirit. A second century prologue to the Gospel of Luke provided this epitaph for the good doctor: "He served the Lord without distraction, having neither wife nor children, and at the age of 84 he fell asleep in Boeotia, full of the Holy Spirit."[8] How perfectly fitting.

Remember, God is a giver. In the riveting words of Romans 8:32, "He who did not spare his own Son but gave him up for us all, how will he not also with him graciously give us all things?" (ESV). We could testify to temporal gifts God has given us until our voices are hoarse, but the sum of them pales in comparison to the supreme gift of Christ's own Spirit. In this one present, we spend a lifetime unwrapping endless others: His comforts, His joys, His appointments, His empowerments, His directions, His affections. To these there is no end.

In the words of Christ to the Samaritan woman,

"if you only knew the gift God has for you ... you would ask me ..."

JOHN 4:10, NLT

First Corinthians 2:12 reads, "Now we have not received the spirit of the world, but the Spirit who comes from God, so that we may understand what has been freely given to us by God." Write a prayer asking God to increase your awe and understanding regarding what His Spirit can do even in these next few minutes. Ask Him to break through barriers of overfamiliarity with any of the concepts.

Record God's exact words about His Spirit in the following verses:

Ezekiel 36:27

Zechariah 4:6

Luke 4:18

Tell Him if any of those land on you with personal significance right now and why.

Read Exodus 35:30-35 and recount to God the kind of unction He gave through His Holy Spirit.

Read Acts 9:31 and be bold enough to ask Him to multiply the church similarly today.

Return to Luke 11:13 in conclusion. Note the one glorious condition to receiving the "how much more" God is willing to give of the Holy Spirit: ASK. Hear His words fall upon your ears like they fell upon those of the Samaritan woman. "If you only knew the gift God has for you ... you would ask Me ..." (John 4:10, NLT). Ask Him, Beloved. And tell Him why you want Him and where you need Him.

The grace of the Lord Jesus Christ, and the love of God, and the fellowship of the Holy Spirit be with you all.

2 CORINTHIANS 13:13

Take a moment and reflect on your quest so far. Look back over each day of study and journal a brief note about what spoke to you, what you learned, and what course corrections you need to make. Then, spend a moment in prayer, writing from your heart to the Lord as you move forward on this quest.

DAY 1

Truths I encountered:

What I learned about myself and Jesus:

Course corrections I need to make:

DAY 2

Truths I encountered:

What I learned about myself and Jesus:

Course corrections I need to make:

DAY 3

Truths I encountered:

What I learned about myself and Jesus:

Course corrections I need to make:

DAY 4

Truths I encountered:

What I learned about myself and Jesus:

Course corrections I need to make:

DAY 5

Truths I encountered:

What I learned about myself and Jesus:

Course corrections I need to make:

Lord, as I move forward ...

Two

Video and audio sessions available for purchase at LifeWay.com/TheQuest.

#QuestStudy

2.1

Every excursion has a launch point. Your previous week involved several questions intended, first and foremost, to facilitate dialogue with God and, second, to help you evaluate your starting position. In geographical terms, Week One was your grid. Your answers to the questions served as horizontal and vertical lines of sorts, intersecting to pinpoint your present location. The lovely thing about a trek with God is that no place is the wrong place for a relaunch. Furthermore, you don't need a dramatic reason for a fresh launch. All it requires is a desire to increase your attentiveness to God on your next stretch of ground. For example, I practice a form of this every January 1st when I crack open a brand new journal. I begin with a letter to God reflecting on the last year and expressing hopes in Him for the next. I make it official on purpose. A fresh start with a soft launch is soon lost.

In an Olympic 100-meter dash, the sound of a prop pistol marks the launch. An air horn signals the start of a marathon. In the Scriptures, our pilgrimage or race of faith starts and restarts no less officially. It consists of neither pistol shot nor air horn. It is a voice command issued by the Commissioner: *GO*. On occasion we get an on-your-mark, get-set, go, but, if you're like me, much of the time you have no idea where your mark is and you are not remotely set. God just says, *GO*.

The verb *go* is found in the Christian Standard Bible 863 times. That is a considerable amount of going. In contrast, the word *stay* can be found around 232 times. Not quite so much staying. In Genesis 1:3 God said "Let there be light." He did not tell the light to go. He told the light to be. But, ironically, when He created human beings, there would be all manner of human goings. From the time man was driven out of the garden in Genesis 3, he has been on the go. Mercifully, every "go" ordained by God for His covenant people has been in one way or another—by design or detour, by exploration or exile, by conquest or commission—to get them back to Himself.

By no coincidence God initiated a new era of faith in both the Old Testament and the New by opening His mouth with the emphatic order, *GO*. Search both launches, keeping an eye out for comparisons.

Every "go" ordained by God for His covenant people has been in one way or another to get them *back to Himself.*

Read Genesis 12:1-9. What did God tell Abram (a.k.a. Abraham) to do?

What were the broader benefits of Abram's obedience? (Gen. 12:3)

How would Abram know where to go? (Gen. 12:1)

How did Abram journey according to Genesis 12:9?

Now read Matthew 28:16-20. What command was issued?

Who issued this command and to whom?

Compare Matthew 28:16-20 to Genesis 12:1-9 and list every possible parallel you can find.

Acts 1:6-11 offers more specifics regarding Christ's instructions in Matthew. Record the geographical locations Jesus gave the disciples in Acts 1:8 and place forward-pointing arrows between them.

The complicated thing about God's command to go is that you may be clueless about where you're going. Such was the case with Abram.

By faith Abraham, when he was called, obeyed and set out for a place that he was going to receive as an inheritance. He went out, even though he did not know where he was going.
HEBREWS 11:8

We are called to similar obedience. We "set out." Like Abraham, we plod this sod by faith. Unlike Abraham, at least we know where we'll finally land, but we have no idea what our journey will entail in the meantime. And, frankly, we're afraid time will be mean. The disciples recognized from the geography in Acts 1:8 that their witness would start where they were and then reverberate like sound waves further and further from home. But as for specifics about the journey? God would employ the same method He used with Abraham: He'd show them. You can behold the process throughout the Book of Acts. He led them in all sorts of ways and often through means finite rationale would call a default.

Read Acts 8:1-5 and describe what God used to scatter the seed of the gospel.

Follow Me, Jesus said. For those of us this side of Christ's ascension, following involves being led by the Spirit (Gal. 5:16-18,25)—the soundless version of "I will show you." Talk about margin for error. Planting ourselves in Christ with His words planted in us is paramount for navigating our path (John 15:7). Without His words we can't test what we discern when our directions at crossroads are unclear. But, you see, our predecessors got it wrong at times, too. They misunderstood the means. The timing. Took matters into their own hands. Mission has always been messy, and yet engaging faltering humans in a holy venture is how God still chooses to fulfill His agenda. And He gets it done.

Contemplate the copious comings and goings for Christ followers. Sometimes the terms are even used in tandem: Circle each "come" and "go."

As you go, announce this: "The kingdom of heaven has come near."

Matthew 10:7, HCSB

And [Jesus] said to them, "Let's go on to the neighboring villages so that I may preach there too. This is why I have come."

Mark 1:38

In the previous verse, Jesus said He had come so He could go (preach). As He neared the cross, He then said He would go so He could come (back):

If I go away and prepare a place for you, I will come back and receive you to Myself, so that where I am you may be also.

JOHN 14:3, HCSB

Christ had no intention of leaving them or us without divine presence as we await His visible appearing.

Nevertheless, I am telling you the truth. It is for your benefit that I go away, because if I don't go away the Counselor will not come to you. If I go, I will send Him to you.

JOHN 16:7, HCSB

Jesus who said "come to me" in Matthew 11:28 said to the same people "Go make disciples" in Matthew 28:19. The most significant part? "Remember, I am with you always, to the end of the age" (v. 20). The gospel has not yet reached the ends of the earth, and it is not yet the end of the age. We are part of the continuance.

Multilayered works of God are ever underway with each of us. In the wake of Christ's walk, we come to go and go to come. We'll see this in our quest. To receive the invitation to come to Jesus is to be under commission to go out and make disciples. You are summoned to your own pilgrimage, walking out your own faith, going from glory to glory on the way to your destination, and, simultaneously, you're meant to ferry the gospel through your witness. He who works in you works through you. Every generation of believers runs the next leg of the race to carry the name of Jesus to the ends of the earth. But not one individual gets lost in the crowd. What He said to all, He says to each—"Remember, I am with you."

God sets the pace. He won't always move you in step with your fellow sojourners. Sometimes you'll feel like you're getting left behind. Other times you'll feel like you're leaving them behind. That's just it. Going always involves some measure of leaving.

For us English speakers, spotting the *go* in the word *gospel* is easy. What is less obvious is the *go* in *grow*.

A stirring scene takes place in Genesis 16 containing a question that will spark today's dialogue. Read Genesis 16:1-8. Record the question the angel of the Lord asked Hagar in verse 8.

In that one glorious moment, the angel of the Lord spun three segments of time into play: Hagar's present (in the wilderness by a spring of water), Hagar's past (where have you come from?), and Hagar's future (where are you going?). Her response would not be for his benefit. He was well acquainted with her biography. His intent was to engage in a dialogue that would goad a different epilogue. God is equally acquainted with your biography. Still, articulating your version of your story to Him can posture you for hints of His story for you.

In Week One, you documented your present. Today you set your compass toward where you are going. However, before that, would you tell God where you've come from? Your backstory doesn't need to be articulated dramatically or even redemptively. You are still en route. It's just the two of you. Tell Him.

Read Genesis 16:9-12, and record the command and promise the angel of the LORD gave to Hagar.

God sent Hagar back to the same location but not as the same hopeless woman. She carried the promise of propagation in her future. God may keep you indefinitely in the same place, but if you walk with Him you cannot remain the same person. There is still the going.

If you walk with *Him*, you cannot remain the *same person*.

The moving away from who you once were.

The moving ahead to who God wants you to be.

The moving away from what you once did and not just the foolish and fleshly things. Sometimes, the good and brilliant and admirable things can make for harder goodbyes. Our temptation to linger among the victories, to relive them, to recreate or duplicate them is titanic.

Is there something you did before that you keep trying to do again? Express it to God.

Sometimes a previous spiritual awakening is what we long to re-experience. You can grab an old book that God used powerfully in your past. Only, this time, He doesn't meet you there the same way.

Does this sound familiar? Recount it here.

Like the Israelites who were to look to the cloudy pillar over the tabernacle to determine their going or staying, sometimes we're all settled in when God seems to pick up and move on. His Spirit doesn't depart from within us, of course, but He's leading us onward. If we don't move on when He does, we're left with old images of flames that have lost their heat. No amount of rubbing sticks together can spark holy fire. It comes from the Spirit alone. The only book that can spring to life for the thousandth time is the one with His breath on it.

Should God keep you within a ten-mile radius for years on end, there is still the going. Like this mountainous planet, we have a mountainous spiritual terrain. Every traveler climbs heights and plunges to depths. As long as you have a pulse, your timeline won't be a flatline. Welcome to the electrocardiogram journey of the beloved child of God. He has a title that matches your three segments of time.

As long as you have a *pulse*, your timeline won't be a flatline.

Write the title He gives Himself in Revelation 1:8 and view how the references to time correspond to the statement below it:

"I am the Alpha and the Omega," says the Lord God,
"the one … ______________, ______________, and ____________________ …"

"Almighty" for where you are, where you have been, and where you are going.

Fill in the blanks to close:

From Matthew 28:20 - "And remember, __________________________ always."

From Genesis 16:13 - "She gave this name to the LORD who spoke to her:
'____'" (NIV).

2.2

This expedition will camp you next to Abraham on several occasions because he is the unrivaled archetype for the walk of faith. Our commonalities with him are legion. For starters, Abraham didn't choose God. God chose him. The same is true for us.

Abraham was called to go and so are we.

He had no idea where and neither do we.

He was enormously blessed and so are we.

He had divine promises over his life and so do we.

He thought God was taking too long and so have we.

He tried to fulfill a miraculous plan with natural means and so have we.

He took matters into his own hands with resultant heartache. And so have we.

God's engagement with Abraham also provided the grounds for one of Scripture's most remarkable doctrines. This doctrine has momentous impact on the quality if not the pure bearability of our earthly quests. Connect some Old and New Testament dots to draw it forth.

Read Genesis 15:1-6. Write verse 6 here.

Please take a moment and let those words sink in, even—and perhaps especially —if the concept is familiar to you. It strikingly counters our human reasoning. Our natural tendency is to calculate a person's righteousness by his or her righteous acts. What, after all, does faith have to do with righteousness? To God, everything.

Read and savor Romans 4:1-25. What connection is made between Genesis 15 and Romans 4 in Romans 4:22-25?

Push past the chapter break and read Romans 5:1-5. How has this miracle of peace with an unprofaned God happened for people like me—like you—who are fraught with sin?

To feel the force of this grace personally, insert "I" in the blanks of Romans 5:6-10, where the Scripture reads "we."

For while [____ was] still helpless, at the right time, Christ died for the ungodly. For rarely will someone die for a just person—though for a good person perhaps someone might even dare to die. But God proves his own love for [me] in that while [____ was still a sinner], Christ died for [me]. How much more then, since [___] have now been declared righteous by his blood, will [____] be saved through him from wrath. For if, while we were enemies, we were reconciled to God through the death of his Son, then how much more, having been reconciled, will [___] be saved by his life.

Did you catch the three-word phrase comprising our fifth recalibrating question? It popped up twice. Circle both.

Return to Genesis 15 and read verses 7-21. In this stunning narrative, God responds to Abraham's question in verse 8 by presenting a formal treaty that would rest entirely on God's unwavering faithfulness. The visuals God involved are striking. "Most agree that the smoking firepot and burning torch represent the Lord, a picture corresponding to the pillar of cloud and pillar of fire indicating the presence of God in the wilderness."[1] The sacrificial shedding of blood was required first just as it would be four hundred years later in the Mosaic law, each sacrifice foreshadowing the death of Christ, the perfect and final sacrifice. Centuries later at a Passover table on the evening of His arrest, Christ presented the new covenant that He'd ratify with His own blood before the next sundown.

When the hour came, he reclined at the table, and the apostles with him. Then he said to them, "I have fervently desired to eat this Passover with you before I suffer. For I tell you, I will not eat it again until it is fulfilled in the kingdom of God." Then he took a cup, and after giving thanks, he said, "Take this and share it among yourselves. For I tell you, from now on I will not drink of the fruit of the vine until the kingdom of God comes." And he took bread, gave thanks, broke it, gave it to them, and said, "This is my body, which is given for you. Do this in remembrance of me." In the same way he also took the cup after supper and said, "This cup is the new covenant in my blood, which is poured out for you."

LUKE 22:14-20

Circle back to my earlier suggestion that faith counted as righteousness can have a momentous impact on the ____________________ if not the pure ________________________ of our earthly quests. I write these next words to you with great affection and tremendous empathy as one who rarely learns a hefty thing an easy way.

If you bear the responsibility for your worthiness to traverse with God and try to maintain an A+ in righteousness, you will collapse. You may stay steady on your feet long enough to assume some credit, but soon your knees will buckle and the credit will topple from your hands. It's too weighty to carry. Self-righteousness even for Jesus' sake will finally make roadkill of you. The devil is too clever and well acquainted with your blind spots for you to get away with it indefinitely.

You may not tumble into the kinds of grievous sins that I did, but you will sprawl into exhaustion and numbness or sink into the quicksand of legalism and pride. You will also set yourself up for a shocking crisis when, inevitably along the way, your righteousness does not turn into the imminent reward you expected. The fact is, sometimes doing the right thing can temporarily lead to the most pain. It may mean forfeiting a relationship or an opportunity or losing a job over an unwillingness to compromise (1 Pet. 3:14). A theology that says, if I do the right thing, God will always do the right thing (i.e. make me happy) is consequentially shortsighted. He never fails to do the right thing, but far more is in play in our earthly quests than our temporal felicity.

Make no mistake, happiness beyond human vocabulary awaits us on the other side of the veil. It can peek out from behind the curtain at times, spiking our joy and comforting us with foretastes of heaven. However, though we rightly pursue righteousness, it doesn't flip a happiness switch. Right decisions will always lead to blessing, but sometimes it is a long trip. Here's what we don't have to wait for: victory. I'm a woman of no few years and have come to embrace victory as its own brand of felicity. Expect more on that subject as we go.

The following questions need early answers in our quest with God: 1) Whose worthiness is this walk based upon? 2) Whose promises are keeping this relationship afoot?

Christ will keep His covenant promises to us by His own righteousness—a righteousness He ascribed to the fallen when He bore the full weight of our wrongs on the cross. Our part is to believe. Our part is to place our faith in the finished work of Christ for our unfinished lives. This is what He counts as righteousness. Talk of this kind can make people nervous because they fear it leads to licentiousness, but that's the mysterious turnabout. We can't walk in fiery faith and remain in a mire of sin. Our feet will follow our faith. It's faith that gives us the guts to change. It's faith that snaps lengthy chains of poor decisions. It's faith that upturns a downward spiral. Because, my friend, "This is the victory that has conquered the world: our faith" (1 John 5:4).

Abraham is not only the archetype for the walk of faith. His relationship with God is Exhibit A for the claim that questions are intrinsic in any true quest.

Search Genesis 15:1-8 for two questions Abraham asked God and record where they are found: verse _____ and verse _____.

Abraham had a highly unique relationship with God in large part because he heard God's voice. Let these two facts be a comfort to you: 1) Abraham still had questions even though God had spoken audibly. 2) Abraham felt the freedom to ask them. Your relationship with God has its own distinctions. No matter how many children a caring parent has, each child bears uniqueness. If your relationship with God is active and fully engaged, you've no doubt experienced angst in trying to understand His ways. Perhaps you have your own personalized forms of the questions Abraham asked God in verses 2 and 8.

Meditate on these blanks representing the first question, but don't fill them in just yet.

Genesis 15:2 - Lord GOD, what can you give me, since I am
_______________ and ____
_________________?

You can sense the depth of the ache in the New Living Translation of the scene:

> **But Abram replied, "O Sovereign LORD, what good are all your blessings when I don't even have a son? Since you've given me no children, Eliezer of Damascus, a servant in my household, will inherit all my wealth. You have given me no descendants of my own, so one of my servants will be my heir."**
>
> **GENESIS 15:2-3**

Haven't you felt that kind of frustration or disappointment at some point in your life? Most of the time you are well aware that God's blessings are gloriously good and beneficial whether or not you are receiving what you want most from God or what you believe He's promised you. But, if you're like most people on an active faith walk, sometimes you've felt that all else means little without the one thing you most long for. Perhaps this is currently where you are. Or maybe you remember a time when you felt exactly this way.

Whether you recount a previous time in your faith walk or a very present struggle, go back and fill in those blanks for Genesis 15:2, and then talk to Him about them here.

Perhaps the following words wrap language around something you need to articulate to your very gracious God: *Lord, You've given me so much and I am deeply grateful, but You have not given me the thing I have long believed the purpose for my life hinges on.*

If these words resonate, expound on this to God.

Have you wrestled internally, feeling like you've tried to live righteously, tried to do the right things, but God somehow still hasn't come through? Few people will bypass this struggle. Give voice to it here, and, if you're willing, commit toward walking forward in faith even in the midst of frustration.

After restating the promise to Abraham in Genesis 15:4, please note what God did. "He took him outside and said, 'Look at the sky …'" (v. 5). Abraham was in his tent when the word of the Lord came to him. It is moving that God escorted Abraham outside the limited perimeters of his manmade tent to expand his vision. Sometimes the faith walker stares too long at the cramped walls of his or her own understanding and needs to be escorted outside where he or she can see the wide-open sky and be challenged to think bigger.

Is it possible that your vision is too limited and your faith has been indoors, so to speak, far too long? Express your response to God.

Now glance back at Genesis 15:7-8 and focus on four words: *How can I know?* Abraham received an answer. Simply put, *I will make an unbreakable covenant with you that I will be faithful to.* Please don't miss that the answer came bloodily and dramatically and that God placed Abraham in a deep sleep probably so the man could survive the theophany. You may wonder what this has to do with you, but the peculiarity is that you've received an answer similar to the one God gave to Abraham. In the stirring words of 1 Thessalonians 4:14, "if we believe that Jesus died and rose again, in the same way, through Jesus ..." Beloved, if God can raise the crucified, dead, and buried back to life on the third day is there anything He cannot do?

2.3

The concept for this six-week quest is breathtakingly conspicuous in the relationship God invited Abraham to embrace. That relationship earns substantial ink this week. Abraham's entire narrative is a captivating case study for the life of faith, but we have a specific agenda narrowing our lens. Sticking to the task, we are making stops at three different locations in the Abrahamic narrative where questions come dramatically into play between an old tent-dweller and his eternal God.

Read Genesis 17:1–18:15, and record every question that pops up in the text and who presents it. I'll get you started.

REFERENCE	INQUIRER	QUESTION
Gen. 17:17	Abraham	Can a child be born to a hundred-year-old man?

We've arrived at a strategic spot on the map where a vertical line and a horizontal line intersect to mark the makings of sacred intimacy. Intimacy with God is not like intimacy between people. No passage of time or earthly erosion can green the gleam of "the Son of God, the one whose eyes are like a fiery flame and whose feet are like fine bronze" (Rev. 2:18). Overfamiliarity masquerades as mastery but, in truth, always betrays a lack of intimacy with God. Overfamiliarity confuses godly things with God Himself. Gratefully, we can relax in His presence and rest in His comfort and peace. He is home to us. We find leisure at His feet for our overworked bodies and rough and tumbled souls. We have safe exposure in our full disclosure. But He is not our counterpart. We echoed early in our launch that God has no peer, yet we will soon see, lest we think we've got Him pegged, that He does have friends.

Genesis 17 documents two separate times Abraham fell on his face: verses _____ and _____.

The terminology indicates Abraham did not simply go to his face. He "fell facedown." Somewhere between those two verses, he came either to his knees or feet only to fall facedown again. I think perhaps we've stumbled onto one of Abraham's few contributions to the sacred relationship he enjoyed with God: his knees buckled easily. He never forgot that God was God and he was not.

Abraham's awe for God did not stop him from bringing his questions to God. It escorted him. Fear of the Lord was footwear in his quest with the One who could roar, "I am God Almighty. Live in my presence and be blameless" (Gen. 17:1). Abraham's facedown reverence spoke a wordless language of worship. Abraham laughed at the thought that he and Sarah could still conceive. But make no mistake, he did so with his face in the dirt.

One little word is luminous in Abraham's cackling question. Fill it in the blank.

Then he laughed and said to himself, "Can a child be born to a hundred-year-old man? Can _________________, a ninety-year-old woman, give birth?"

He spoke her new name immediately, even in words to himself. In the very same breath he brought questions, he breathed faith. Feeling conflicted and confused is not the same as faithlessness. It takes faith to wrestle with doubt.

God is remarkably patient with the inquiries of man in the Bible; however, we're mistaken to think being questioned never raised His ire (Luke 5:21-22). I believe it's possible that Abraham's horizontal attitude—facedown—had significant impact on his vertical access—face up.

What comes prodigiously to light in Genesis 17 and 18 is that God reserves the right to reveal Himself however He pleases. This may seem for now a passing observation, but it could not be further removed from one. It is, instead, an impasse of sorts. To embrace this One with whom we walk we must find security in His identity rather than His predictability. This entire course is a lesson in learning to trust God enough to appreciate, if not unabashedly delight in, His exercised right to retain mystery. According to His self-disclosure in Exodus 34:6-7, we can be utterly certain "Yahweh is a compassionate and gracious God, slow to anger and rich in faithful love and truth, maintaining faithful love to a thousand generations, forgiving wrongdoing, rebellion, and sin" (HCSB), but we cannot always predict how He will reveal those traits to us personally or to humanity generally.

> "Obscurity is story's way of telling us the truth about this God with whom we daily have to do, by reminding us of God's hiddenness, of the concreteness of God's revelation and of the *impossible possibilities* that are open to all who believe."
>
> W. M. ALSTON[2]

Genesis 17:1 opens with a classic theophany. Thirteen years had passed between the last verse of Genesis 16 and the first verse of Genesis 17. "The LORD appeared to him," but no clues are given regarding what Abraham actually saw. From the reader's perspective, God revealed Himself in the scene primarily through proclamation. Then "when he finished talking with him, God withdrew from Abraham" (Gen. 17:22).

The next thing we know, "The LORD appeared to Abraham" while he was likely napping through the midday heat at the entrance to his tent (Gen. 18:1). With cinematic timing, the old man blinked his eyes wide open to a party of three. Mind you, this scene is only eighteen chapters into the entire Bible. Bible students who shun the supernatural are forced to tiptoe around Scriptures such as this like they're navigating a live minefield. God is not interested in playing by our rules or stoking our always-and-nevers. His Majesty does what His Majesty wants. Let this become cause for celebration rather than consternation.

Abraham again bowed to the ground, but whether or not he had fully perceived a divine visitation is unknown. Though there were three, he addressed only one: "My lord, if I have found favor with you …" (v. 3). The word "lord" (*aḏōnāy*) is a title of respect that can be used for any superior, whether man or God, and differs from the term found in many major translations in all uppercase letters: "LORD" (*yhwh*). This name is reserved for God alone. What is clear, however, is that Abraham was most anxious to host the entourage and zealously encouraged them to tarry. Not only would the meal have taken hours to prepare (from herd to savory roast!), the measure of flour would have produced a volume of bread exceeding what three men could eat. Abraham knew these were no ordinary guests.

The man, sleepy and sluggish just moments ago, broke into a full run in the heat of the day to fetch dinner. He then spread a feast before the trio, and, as they dined, he served as "both waiter and host."[3] Taste this morsel: "In OT thought God inhales the pleasing odor of sacrifice, but he does not consume the sacrifice. Surely it is not without significance that only when Yahweh is in the guise of a wayfarer does he partake of food (18:8; 19:3)."[4]

How can you know for certain this was a divine visitation? Cite any verse in Genesis 18:1-15 that offers proof.

Our temptation to interpret the three visitors as the Trinity may be compelling, but Genesis 19 steers elsewhere, blowing away the cloud over their identity. Rather than Father, Son, and Holy Spirit, the trio turns out to be God and two of His angels (Gen. 19:1). The intrigue is enormous. Scan a range of possibilities through these verses. Record any pertinent information.

Exodus 25:22

Isaiah 37:16

John 20:11-14

Sarah's contribution to the scene is gold. How gracious and patient is a God who speaks not only with His hearers in mind but with His overhearers, too? You no doubt noticed she laughed and not facedown. She cackled at the absolute absurdity of the pregnancy prospect and the Lord called her out in a delightfully brow-raising tête–à–tête.

So she laughed to herself …

"Why did Sarah laugh … ?"

Sarah denied it. "I did not laugh," she said, because she was afraid.

But he replied, "No, you did laugh."

But there she still stood. No lightning strike. No pillar of salt. No sudden outbreak of leprosy. The earth did not quake and swallow her whole. The Lord confronted her, but He did not condemn her. So why did He make such an issue of her laughter beyond the obvious notation of her lack of faith? Could it be that He wanted that word *laughter* to stick? Could it be that He meant for the old couple to replay that word again and again in the next twelve months? In Genesis 17:19 God told Abraham the child was to be called Isaac, a name meaning, "he laughed."[5] It would not be a thorny reminder of an old couple's doubt. It would be a deliciously sweet endearment, born of a God who is ridiculously good. Glance ahead to Genesis 21:1-7 and enjoy.

Write Sarah's words in Genesis 21:6 here:

Compare Genesis 17:17 and 18:12. Please don't miss that both Abraham and Sarah pointed out not just one but two strikes against them regarding conception. The prospect was a double impossibility. With much care and attentiveness, reread Romans 4:16-25, pausing at verse 19 to see the turnabout in Abraham's faith regarding the double impossibility.

What has God done for you that, had someone said it to you years ago, you would have laughed? Or perhaps someone actually did suggest it and you did indeed laugh. Remember it with Him by writing to Him.

Now shift your thoughts from what would have been laughable in the past to what would be laughable now. What wonder did you hope for in the past that is so ridiculously impossible now, it's laughable? Whether God still intends to fulfill it (literally or spiritually) or it wasn't His plan and has long-since been off the table, He's still at the table. It is part of your history with Him. Recall it to Him.

The name *Isaac* means *laughter*. You have your own Isaacs, spiritually speaking. You've had times when your laughter has come full circle from that which seemed ridiculous to that which became such a gift that words hardly sufficed. All you could do was throw your head back and laugh in wonder how God could be so patient and good. If an example comes to mind, tell Him about it.

With one divine question came the glorious confluence of correction, conviction, confirmation, and unfettered hope. Write God's question in Genesis 18:14 here.

2.4

Today the quest will take you around the final bend in Abraham's narrative. And in terms of our concept, it will be a grand finale indeed. Return to Genesis 18. Review and recapture the mood of verses 1-15, and then read verses 16-33. As it turns out, the three visitors had two purposes for their journey rather than just one.

Describe the stark contrast between their stopover at Abraham's and where they next set their sights.

Abraham continued in the role of attentive host, accompanying his guests on the first leg of their journey. The Lord then spoke either to Himself or to His two emissaries, presumably in such a way that Abraham would overhear (Gen. 18:17-21). The juxtaposition of the laughter in the previous scene and the outcry in the present scene is jarring and not to be missed. Isn't that the way of the earth? A cacophony of truth, laughter, hopes, hurts, deceptions, death rattles, and horrors of sin? In the last twenty-four hours alone I've thrown my head back and laughed at the antics of the toddler in my arms, but also dropped my head and mourned over unspeakable violence to a child close to her age. Some block an eye to the world's despair to stay focused on the positives, while some block an eye to the world's pleasures to stay focused on the negatives. We need to be people with both eyes open. What was true for Abraham will be true for us: walking with God will be the only way we can successfully manage the polarity in our range of vision.

Record the question the Lord asked in Genesis 18:17.

Give careful attention to the way God expressed His logic in Genesis 18:19. Abraham was to "command his children and his house after him to keep the way of the LORD by doing" exactly what?

The Bible attests to God's omniscience—His complete knowledge—so, at first blush, a verse like Genesis 18:21 can come across as contradictory. If God already knew whether or not the outcry against Sodom and Gomorrah was justified, why did He need to "go down to see"? The preceding three verses bring one reason to light. Remember, Abraham would command generations to keep the way of the LORD by doing what was right and just. There, overlooking a city rife with evil, God gave Abraham a tutorial he would likely never forget. In short, go see with your eyes before you judge with your mouth. In this stirring anthropomorphism, God allowed Abraham to walk with Him so He could teach Abraham how to walk like Him.

What happens next is one of the most moving dialogues between man and God documented in the entire canon. It becomes startlingly clear at this point in Genesis 18 that Abraham well knows the identity of the One standing next to him. And, well knowing, "Abraham stepped forward and said, 'Will you really sweep away the righteous with the wicked?'" (v. 23). Two audacious themes rise high on the edge of that outstretched plain: God dared to confide in Abraham, and Abraham dared to intercede for Sodom.[6]

The intertwining of Abraham's boldness and humility is as arresting. Record evidence of each in the rest of Genesis 18.

BOLDNESS	HUMILITY

In order to let the dialogue sink a little deeper into your memory, list the numbers Abraham offered in his inquiry of how many righteous inhabitants might be required for God to spare the city.

There are moments in Scripture of such epic proportions that we turn to them again and again, whether literally with our fingers thumbing through pages or mentally through recollections of the scene. Some of them are unusually brief for their weightiness and strangely unique in what they offer to the sacred script. The scene recorded in Luke 23:39-43 is one of those for me. Jesus hung on a cross between two thieves who'd received the same death sentence. One used what little breath he had left to heave his chest and hurl insults at Jesus.

"Aren't you the Messiah? Save yourself and us!"

But the other answered, rebuking him: "Don't you even fear God, since you are undergoing the same punishment? We are punished justly, because we're getting back what we deserve for the things we did, but this man has done nothing wrong." Then he said, "Jesus, remember me when you come into your kingdom!"

LUKE 23:39b-42

Jesus' response to the guilty man moves me as much today as it did the first time I really heard it.

"I assure you, today you will be with me in paradise."

LUKE 23:43, NLT

No one can take that scene from us. No one can erase those lines from the page. No one can strip us of that one thread of hope that, in the death of an unsaved loved one, something destiny-changing feasibly could have happened between the dying one and the saving One before the final breath. Slender though that hope may be, it can at times be just thick enough for the grieving who'd prayed and pled for the person's salvation to hang onto. God was unspeakably merciful to give us that moment. The improbable is no harder for God to accomplish than the probable.

The scene between God and Abraham in Genesis 18:23-33 is also a stand-alone of sorts, with effects of epic proportions. By God's own deliberation and inspiration, the scene raises a question early in Scripture that He knew the soul of virtually every person of faith would eventually erupt to ask. He saw to it that the question would be put in plainspoken words requiring little interpretation.

Write the question in Genesis 18:25 in this space below and in all uppercase letters if it helps.

If a Christian can have an existential crisis, doesn't it often go something like this?

Is this One in whom I've placed my faith even good? Will this One around whom I've formed my entire worldview do right by the world? What if this One whom I have trusted isn't trustworthy? What if God is just the lesser of two evils?

Here's a really treacherous one: *What if God really is God—all powerful, completely sovereign, utterly in charge—but He's not perfect after all? What if He has a mean streak?*

Are You mean, Lord? Or are You just unaware? Are You willing but unable? Or able but unwilling? Are Your hands dirty, or are they just tied?

For all of us and for all the times our throats ache to ask, God provoked a question from the mouth of Abraham: "Will not the Judge of all the earth do right?" (Gen. 18:25, NIV).

And God, in an awe-striking display of patience, answered.

Yes.

Who affects You more, Lord: the many wicked or the few righteous? With every subtraction, God offered Abraham an answer: the righteous. "His dialogue with Abraham exhibits the exceptional condescension of God who appears as a man, hears out a man (Abraham), and then ultimately saves a man (Lot)."[7] In a judgment similar to the one over the whole earth in the days of Noah, God removed the righteous from Sodom and brought judgment upon the rest.

And herein lies the conundrum. You and I both know the innocent suffer with the guilty here on this sin-pocked planet. Often in the short run, the innocent suffer instead of the guilty. Further, they often suffer at the hands of the guilty. This is true today and has been true throughout most of human history. The psalmists lamented the same conditions. For crying out loud, God Himself lamented the same conditions calling the people to righteousness, justice, and mercy through the prophets.

God sees.

He hears the cries of the oppressed. The tormented. The abused.

He does not miss a single act of the wicked.

He does not ignore a single intercession.

And the clock is ticking.

God will right every wrong. What is not sorted out here and now will be sorted out then and there. The reckoning. The righteous Judge will do right. He cannot do otherwise. The singular reason why a sinful man like Abraham had it within him and sinful people like you and me have it within us to insist on what is right is because we were created in the image of Him who is righteousness. Every shred of decency we have, every ounce of mercy, every drop of blood we'd willingly shed for freedom and justice for all is the outworking of the interwoven *imago Dei*. The image of God.

Run off to meet Jesus. Tell him the problem. Ask him why he didn't come sooner, why he allowed that awful thing to happen. And then be prepared for a surprising response. I can't predict what the response will be, for the very good reason that it is always, always a surprise. But I do know the shape that it will take. Jesus will meet your problem with some new part of God's future that can and will burst into your present time, into the mess and grief, with good news, with hope, with new possibilities.

N. T. WRIGHT[8]

You may not have the benefit of the Lord walking beside you visibly in the form of flesh and blood as Abraham did in Genesis 18, but Jesus has promised never to leave you nor forsake you. Though your eyes cannot see Him, you walk with God in your obedience as surely as Abraham walked with Him to the edge of that vast plain. Nothing could be more appropriate in today's query than the invitation for you to take your vital place in a role of intercessor. Cry out on behalf of three different people groups that presently burden your heart, and ask God to move on their behalf. Name them. Tell God why you are burdened for them and ask Him for specific acts toward them. Try to go beyond general terms like asking God to bless them or help them. What kinds of ways would you rejoice to see Him work among them? Intercede with the immensely powerful blend of complete boldness and humility.

You have poured out intercession. And true intercession is costly, time-consuming, and often depleting. Now let God pour His words into you to quicken you, comfort you, assure you, and equip you. Read each of the segments below with an eye out for any connection to today's subject matter. You may either record every verse or just the portions that speak most powerfully to you.

Isaiah 51:1-8

Isaiah 58:6-12

Matthew 22:31-32

2.5

You will increasingly notice the needle of your compass pointing to a segment of Scripture that involves aspects of the unexplainable. The atlas on this journey is an intentional guide around blind curves and straight lines to bring certain points into clear view. In thematic terms, you are walking on a path meant to resemble a series of question marks. We have engaged in this quest in part to grapple with and to grow in our acceptance of elements that, this side of eternity, seem utterly unexplainable. But that is not all. Our highest goal exceeds mere acceptance. The dare on this quest is to embolden our appreciation for them. The blanks make space not only for faith, though faith is supreme and "more valuable than gold" (1 Pet. 1:7). The blanks make space for wonder. Wonder is faith caught in a momentary burst of imagination. Wonder slips a fresh slice of childlikeness into a grown-up sojourner's faith.

Fast forward in your Bible now from Genesis 18 to Exodus 33. Just as God foretold to Abraham in Genesis 15 through the graphic presentation of covenant, the patriarch's descendants sojourned to Egypt, and, over generations and burgeoning populations, lost favor with the government and were reduced to slaves. The Pharaoh on the throne in the opening pages of Exodus was Scripture's original human trafficker. He placed impossible demands on his slave laborers who, unfortunately for Pharaoh, also happened to be God's chosen people. Moved with compassion by His people's plight, God called Moses from the backside of the desert to return to Egypt and demand their release. After spectacular signs and wonders, significant drama, and a staggering death toll, the Israelites were set free to follow their leader, Moses, into the wilderness to journey toward the promised land. Along the way, God called Moses to the top of Mount Sinai to receive the commandments. Meanwhile, down below, the

Israelites, under the leadership of Aaron, got tired of waiting and danced their way into grievous sin and idolatry. Your reading today picks up in the wake of their rebellion.

Read Exodus 33:1-11. List what God told the Israelites He would do for them in verses 1-3a.

What was the one catch? (v. 3b)

What did the people do when Moses entered the tent to meet with God?

No matter how many times you've heard the concept, let this statement sink deep enough to plunge you into a well of wonder: God makes friends. Abraham was called by the slack-jawing title "a friend of God" in both testaments (Isa. 41:8; Jas. 2:23). The term surfaces again in reference to God's relationship with Moses. Take another close look at the wording in Exodus 33:11. The tendency is to accidentally impose a switch in roles between God and Moses and assume Moses spoke to God as a man speaks to a friend. That, after all, is how many of us are appropriately taught to pray as children—"You can talk to God like He is your friend." But the scene in Exodus 33:11 depicts the reverse. God was the party doing the friend-speak. Try to find a place for that in your imagination.

"The LORD would speak with Moses ______________ to ______________ ..."

EXODUS 33:11a

The chapter later states that Moses could not survive a glimpse of God's face; therefore, the phrase is interpreted as an idiom we could translate "presence to presence." For God's face to "shine upon you" was the ultimate blessing and unabashed bestowal of divine favor. It was the unseen face of God alight with pleasure. Eugene Peterson captures the imagery in his paraphrase of the Hebrew:

GOD spoke to Moses: "Tell Aaron and his sons, This is how you are to bless the People of Israel. Say to them, GOD bless you and keep you, GOD smile on you and gift you, GOD look you full in the face and make you prosper. In so doing, they will place my name on the People of Israel—I will confirm it by blessing them."

NUMBERS 6:22-27 (THE MESSAGE)

"GOD ________________ on you and ______________ you."

Do you struggle to imagine God smiling on you? Whether your answer is yes or no, expound on several reasons why.

Express a specific time when you felt that God may have been smiling on you or taking particular pleasure in you. If you've never felt that way, don't hesitate to say so. Remember, this journey will take us no further than our honesty.

The road ahead will circle back to the concept of God's great pleasure in His children so hold onto it for the duration.

Read Exodus 33:12-23. What did Moses ask God in verse 16?

Survey each of Moses' requests and each of God's corresponding responses in verses 12-17. Record the request and God's wording for each specific yes He gave Moses.

MOSES' REQUEST	GOD'S RESPONSE

Write the words of Moses in Exodus 33:15.

The profoundness of this exchange between God and Moses is difficult to overstate. Thousands of years later, what this dialogue projects about God has the potential to vigorously affect our trek with Him and to wreck some of our pedestrian religion. Review this with me.

God assured Moses at the opening of Exodus 33 that He would keep every promise He'd made to Israel. Despite the gravity of their sin, that plan had not been abandoned. Moses and the people were to arise and set foot toward the promised land. God reconfirmed His steadfast intention for the descendants of Abraham, Isaac, and Jacob to receive covenant real estate and would see to it personally. He guaranteed Moses that he and the people would have a God-appointed angelic escort. And here is the big one: He reassured Moses in no uncertain terms that He would drive out the inhabitants so the Israelites could move into the land flowing with milk and honey.

Angelic accompaniment

Victory

Real estate

Milk and honey

Everything God promised them

There was only one catch:
He wasn't going with them (Ex. 33:3).

Moses' reply? No deal. Then leave us here.

In the desert, mind you.

Allow me a little license to paraphrase: *I'd rather be right here in the thorns and thistles and never know the taste of milk and honey if that's what it takes to have You. Let my foes keep every inch of that land if, in order to possess it, I can't have You. Give me every blessing that I can have and still have You or give me nothing at all besides You. No promise on earth can take the place of Your presence. I choose the desert if that's where You are. If You're not going, I'm staying.*

This is the God whose very presence is in your presence. This is the God who waits for you to acknowledge Him. This is the God who summons you to come meet with Him. This same presence reflected in your life, in your love, your hope, your joy, and, at times, in the pure radiance of your face is your most distinguishing mark on this earth. Talent can't match it. Beauty can't match it. Celebrity can't match it. Romance can't match it. A best seller can't match it. An invention can't match it. A Fortune 500 company can't match it. All the milk and honey on the planet can't match it.

No mansion. No marriage. No van full of car seats. No platform or position. Nothing compares.

If your Presence does not go with us, do not send us up from here.

EXODUS 33:15, NIV

Maybe you haven't had a theophany like those Abraham and Moses experienced. You haven't heard the audible voice of God like they did. You've never seen the God-sparked fire and smoke they saw. You've never beheld God's incomprehensible glory toweled in a cloud. Maybe you've never gotten a single glimpse of anything you could call a bona fide miracle. But let this truth hammer hard and long on the door of your heart until it beats its way in: this God they knew is your God. This God's presence was worth everything to them. Nothing on earth compared to it. They'd tasted and seen. After that, nothing else could suffice. Without the divine presence, a lion's share of divine promises was not enough to distinguish them and carry them. That presence is with you. You aren't Abraham. You aren't Moses. But just one shift will be the catalyst for a life that values exactly the same thing they did. Be present in His presence. Alert. Undistracted. Not just present in the open face of a Bible. Present in the open face of God Himself. He has always been there. Be there, too. This one shift changes everything. Freestyle in your journaling with anything you'd like to say to Him or ask of Him. If you've never experienced God in a compelling way, be brave enough to ask Him to engage you in a relationship that you'd find incomparable.

Read Exodus 33:18-23 and try to imagine the unimaginable. Record Moses' audacious request in verse 18.

God esteems a bold request made in faith and awe. He will bless your faith even if He doesn't grant your full petition. If you have a bold request for God based on today's theme, have courage enough to make it.

The prospect of surrendering fully to the glory of God can be terrifying if you perceive that a mortal can only legitimately glorify God through suffering, hardship, and pain. Simply put, the glory of God is His God-ness. It is that which exalts Him and makes Him conspicuous. God can be glorified in your suffering, but He can also be glorified in your joy. He can be glorified in your weakness, and He can be glorified in your strength.

Fill in the following blanks with words from God's own mouth in Exodus 33:19 and 22.

> "I will cause all my ________________ to pass in front of you, and I will proclaim the name 'the LORD' before you ... and when my ________________ passes by, I will put you in the crevice of the rock and cover you with my hand until I have passed by."

Witness the gorgeous inseparability of God's goodness and glory. He does not suspend His goodness for His glory's sake nor His glory for goodness' sake.

Read 2 Peter 1:3, and tell God what He's done for you according to this solitary verse.

Invite Him to reassure your soul of the goodness of His glory. Share your hesitations about growing closer to Him.

When life feels dreadfully dark and you can't see a single fleck of light, maybe it's not too far a reach to think perhaps God could have you in a crevice covered with His hand. He will be good to you, but it is possible to be blind to His goodness until the blackness has ended. In the wording of Exodus 33:23, sometimes you may only see His back.

Centuries later, human eyes did behold His glory but it was not toweled in a cloud. It was wrapped in porous, bruisable, breakable, touchable, embraceable human skin, fully entered into our vulnerable estate. The apostle John said of Jesus, "We have seen his glory, the glory of the one and only Son, who came from the Father, full of grace and truth" (John 1:14, NIV). "That which was from the beginning, which we have heard, which we have seen with our eyes, which we have looked at and our hands have touched" (1 John 1:1, NIV). God's engagement with Abraham also provided the grounds for one of Scripture's most remarkable doctrines. This doctrine has momentous impact on the quality if not the pure bearability of our earthly quests. Connect some Old and New Testament dots to draw it forth.

Read Genesis 15:1-6. Write verse 6 here.

"The sweetest thing in all my life has been the longing—to reach the Mountain, to find the place where all the beauty came from ... my country, the place where I ought to have been born. Do you think it all meant nothing, all the longing? The longing for home? For indeed it now feels not like going, but like going back."

C. S. LEWIS[9]

Take a moment and reflect on your quest so far. Look back over each day of study and journal a brief note about what spoke to you, what you learned, and what course corrections you need to make. Then, spend a moment in prayer, writing from your heart to the Lord as you move forward on this quest.

DAY 1

Truths I encountered:

What I learned about myself and Jesus:

Course corrections I need to make:

DAY 2

Truths I encountered:

What I learned about myself and Jesus:

Course corrections I need to make:

DAY 3

Truths I encountered:

What I learned about myself and Jesus:

Course corrections I need to make:

DAY 4

Truths I encountered:

What I learned about myself and Jesus:

Course corrections I need to make:

DAY 5

Truths I encountered:

What I learned about myself and Jesus:

Course corrections I need to make:

Lord, as I move forward ...

Three

Video and audio sessions available for purchase at LifeWay.com/TheQuest.

#QuestStudy

3.1

I suspect many of us struggle, and often in vain, to feel like we truly belong. Not long ago I asked a large crowd of people how many of them would own up to feeling like a misfit on a fairly regular basis in several spheres of their lives. I'd hoped for enough hands to make my point. However, what I got was a majority thunderous enough to make the ones who had no such struggle to suddenly feel like—you guessed it—misfits. The irony in our unshakable sense of alienation is that many of us are keeping the exact same secret.

We keep looking for the perfect fit in virtually any category—relationally, vocationally, spiritually, physically—and, every now and then, we may even feel like we've found it. Then something changes. What we thought was a perfect fit eventually starts getting too loose here or too tight there. If you're like me, you wonder with frustration, "Why can't anything stay just-right?" We figure something must have gone wrong that caused the change. And, if we proceed with natural human deductions, soon we wonder whose fault it was and how it can be fixed. If we conclude that it can't be fixed (primarily because so-and-so's fault can't be fixed), we often throw in the towel and look somewhere else and, preferably, for someone new. Sometimes God is at the helm prompting us to move. However, if our only reason for departure is to continue our cyclical search for the perfect fit, we may as well quit while we're ahead.

We search for the ultimate church that meets all our preferences in worship, Word, and companionship, and lo and behold, sometimes we think we've discovered it. Then, just about the time we settle in, disappointment inevitably comes in one area or another and dashes our high hopes into the nearest ditch. We then have a choice: forsake that assembly in search of another, or stick around to see what kind of mosaic Jesus could build with a cooperative bunch of misfit pieces.

Have you ever stuck around with a group of diverse believers and watched Jesus arrange it into a living work of art? Explain.

Our tendency is to view ourselves as puzzle pieces with precise edges looking for perfect fits that comprise perfect portraits. We want every edge met, nipped, and tucked, and every space filled. No two pieces can be left buckling in our ideal image of a healthy church. We'll have that one day, gathered around God's throne, but until then, perhaps nothing testifies to Christ's presence more exquisitely than a willing assemblage of mismatched pieces grouted by grace and grounded in love, exposed to the light of Scripture to make the colors stand out. In the church of Jesus Christ, pieces fit because they're in the same hand, not because they have smooth edges.

In the church of Jesus Christ, pieces fit because they're in the *same hand*.

Our search for a perfect fit is not just social or functional. We both know it is also deeply personal. On the one hand we savor the idea of God-fashioned uniqueness, and on the other hand, we search the world over for someone who shares our every nuance, view, and vision. Some of us—count me in—hear people talk whimsically about their soul mates, and though we've found numerous likes and loves, we always feel like someone is missing. We presume it's our soul mate and wonder why some relationships that come easily to others seem to escape us altogether. We beg and plead of people, place, and thing, "Be what I long for." Some hold great promise but none hold real permanence. We can end up angrier at people who were almost enough than those who were nowhere close. We figure, had the almost-enoughs tried just a little harder, they would have been precisely enough.

Much of this angst resides within people of faith from one worthy cause: we don't belong here. Don't misunderstand. We're meant to be here for now. Literally sent forth here for now, as you'll soon see if you don't already know. But this is not our place of belonging. It became alien to us and we to it the moment we were born again in Christ.

This world is not our home.

If you're like me, you may be quick to nod your head to those familiar words and proceed to the next line of thought. But let's resist a quick getaway this time. Too much is at stake in the way we approach our journeys.

Earlier in the quest you looked at a fascinating chapter of Scripture that allows the reader to eavesdrop on Christ's intercessory prayer for His followers. Return to the same chapter for an additional portion.

Read John 17:1-20 with rapt attention toward every use and detail surrounding the word *world*. List everything Jesus said about the world, specifically in reference to His followers.

We could be depressed by the prospect that we're in a world system where we never quite belong, or we could be relieved. No wonder I often feel like I can't find exactly what I'm looking for. It's not here! Our fear oftentimes is that our relief will descend into dismal resignation that nothing lives up to its press. And resignation can be worse than disappointment. But what if we could step out of the maddening loop of being set up for a let down without rupturing hope or forfeiting every earthly pleasure? Allow me to scribble a few more questions on the chalkboard to churn our imaginations.

What if we discovered that, instead of lowering our expectations, we are meant to set them vastly higher? What if it turned out that our hopes are not too high after all; they're just set to expire too soon? What if we aren't wrong at all to believe in happily-ever-after—it's just that we keep forgetting that our happily-ever is promised after?

Here's the big question that encompasses the rest: What if we truly believed what Christ said we have coming? No one on the planet is at greater risk of experiencing peace and joy than a believer who views the world as a foreign country she serves with love and great purpose, while on her way to some place perfect. Permanent. She's headed to a home where she's never been and one where she'll finally belong.

On any arduous trip, destination is motivation. The anticipation of joy becomes its own joy. It is like making a withdrawal from your inheritance without subtracting a cent from your balance.

The psalmist captured the purview in Psalm 84.

**5 Blessed are those whose strength is in you, whose hearts are set on
pilgrimage. 6 As they pass through the Valley of Baka, they make it a place of
springs; the autumn rains also cover it with pools. 7 They go from strength to
strength, till each appears before God in Zion.**

PSALM 84:5-7, NIV

Circle the name "Zion."

In the *Holman Illustrated Bible Dictionary*, it says: "Zion was used by biblical writers in a variety of ways. Many of the psalmists used the term to refer to the temple built by Solomon (2:6; 48:2; 84:7; 132:13) … The most common usage of Zion was to refer to the city of God in the new age (Isa. 1:27; 28:16; 33:5). Zion was understood, also, to refer to the heavenly Jerusalem (Isa. 60:14; Heb. 12:22; Rev. 14:1), the place where the Messiah would appear at the end of time. The glorification of the messianic community will take place on the holy mountain of 'Zion.'"[1]

To parallel the concept of pilgrimage from a New Testament perspective, record what terms or descriptions pertinent to our discussion are used in reference to Jesus followers in these verses:

1 Peter 1:1

1 Peter 2:11

Hebrews 11:13-14

The New King James Version of Hebrews 11:13-14 uses terminology you don't want to miss.

These all died in faith, not having received the promises, but having seen them afar off were assured of them, embraced them and confessed that they were strangers and pilgrims on the earth. For those who say such things declare plainly that they seek a homeland.

I don't know if you've ever gotten out of bed, stumbled to your lavatory, looked yourself in the mirror and said, "Good morning, Pilgrim," but it might not be a bad idea. I'm willing to try it if you are for "blessed are those … whose hearts are set on pilgrimage."

?

The inspired songwriter referred to the Valley of Baka in Psalm 84. *Baka* poignantly translates *tears*. Go back to Psalm 84:5-7 and rewrite it in first person as a prayer from you to God. The first line is supplied to give you the idea.

Blessed am I when my strength is in You, when my ...

Have you experienced something similar to Psalm 84:6? Has a Valley of Tears ever turned unexpectedly into a place of springs in your pilgrimage with God? If so, recount the season to God and include how you believe the turn took place. If you haven't, freely offer a lament for that valley that remains a memory of nothing but tears. It may not be too late to discover a hidden spring beneath that old wilderness floor.

If you're presently in a Valley of Tears, cry out to God to turn it into a place of springs. Ask Him to show you your part in the transition. The Scripture says "they make it a place of springs" (v. 6), but the context makes clear God alone is their strength. Petition Him for divine strength and the teeming life of the Spirit to see a place of tears turn to springs.

Reflect on the words of Psalm 84:7 "they go from strength to strength." Express to God what you think the psalmist meant.

The very next psalm offers God a question. Write Psalm 85:6 in this space.

Purpose is inherent in the term *pilgrimage*. Allow God to further shape the concept of pilgrimage in your thoughts by seeing how it contrasts to the definition of the word *wander*.

wan•der *wän-dər*\\ verb 1a: to move about without a fixed course, aim, or goal.[2]

Without a destination in mind, walking turns into wandering. Peer into some of the synonyms offered for "wander":

"MEANDER mean[s] to go about from place to place usually without a plan or definite purpose. WANDER implies an absence of or an indifference to a fixed course … ROAM suggests wandering about freely and often far afield … RAMBLE stresses carelessness and indifference to one's course or objective … ROVE suggests vigorous and sometimes purposeful roaming … TRAIPSE implies a course that is erratic but may sometimes be purposeful (*traipsed* all over town looking for the right dress)."[3]

Remember, condemnation has no place in *intimacy* with God.

Remember, condemnation has no place in intimacy with God. Christ bore all condemnation on the cross. When you walk with God and He spotlights a negative pattern, it's always good news. He wants to break the old pattern and cause a victorious one to emerge.

Do any of the previous terms (including *wander*) capture a pattern your journeying tends to take? Tell God about it and what you believe propels it.

In a world of wanderers, you hold a compass. You have a true north. Your path has a God-ordained destination. All it takes for wandering to turn into pilgrimage is a daily destination-orientation. Let the future begin.

3.2

By the time you've been around as long as I have, life has beaten a significant amount of naivety out of you. This is the case as a member of the human race but also as a member of the family of faith. I haven't quite heard it all, but I've heard a lot. I've been steeped like a human tea bag in the warm waters of Christian culture all my life. This is the life I've known most, seen at some of its beautiful best, and tasted at some of its worst. I've been in enough emotionally and spiritually manipulative settings to wince at the first whiff. I can spot the formulas for getting people worked up. I can speak Christianese fluently. I know the politics and the people-pleasing that can run rife. I know the jealousy and rivalry. I know how to exploit Jesus to make myself look good if that's my goal. And, perhaps most painfully, I also know the things that I once believed, then clung to believe, then could no longer believe. I've lost patience with the social media world pinning aphorisms on wounds like dizzy blindfolded children pinning tails on donkeys.

Hemorrhaging naivety can cause all sorts of things to get caught up in the flood and wash away. Gratefully my confidence in the Scriptures has resisted the current. God's Word by His own grace has become increasingly credible to me—solid granite—including stories of one boy's lunch feeding five thousand, filthy lepers healed, and a widow's jar of oil that wouldn't run dry. This morning I fed my next-door donkey an apple, scratched her foot-long ears, and asked myself, "Do you really believe God made one of these talk?" The story seemed absurd in childhood Sunday School, but I've walked a thousand miles with that same unseen God since then. He could have made that donkey sing "I'll Fly Away," then lift off in a cloud of dust, hooves dangling.

> **God's *Word* by His own grace has become increasingly credible to me.**

I make a practice these days of putting myself out there. I risk listening to intelligent people with very different beliefs that oftentimes are no harder to fathom than a virgin birth. I do this because any teacher worth her salt is first and foremost a student. And sheltered communicators are about as useful to their classes as dry milk cows to calves. I've grown up a lot, seen a lot, heard a lot, and experienced a lot, causing simplicity to go the excruciating way of my gullibility. But here I sit, convinced to my partially cynical bones that the reality of this drama—this epic schematic of God's redemption patiently unfolded over several thousand years and meticulously perfected through the gospel of Jesus Christ—so thoroughly exceeds all we can see, touch, and boast that the comparison is almost absurd. We have not made this Bible story up, fellow sojourner. We don't have enough imagination to make it up.

If you are in Christ, you are included in every *our*, *we*, and *us* in the Scriptures below. Document in first person references (I, my, me) any biographical information you can find regarding your life.

Philippians 3:20 ______________________

Colossians 1:13 ______________________

For many of us, these verses inform our theology, but we need more than that for a gospel mentality to make it from the scalps of our heads to the soles of our feet. We can successfully maintain a lifelong doctrinal stand that never interferes with our actual walk. Theology alone can be shelved like a reference book. The preceding verses are not just part of your theology. They describe vivid realities for Jesus followers that much of the unbelieving world would deride as fairy tales.

Once upon a time in a land far away there lived a king's daughter. Few people knew she had royal blood, and she herself often forgot. She'd been born abroad, you see, and had never once been home, but she'd heard about it. She'd read about it. Sometimes she'd even dreamed about it. When she looked in the mirror, she tilted her head and squinted her eyes, struggling to see a princess. The reflection looked more like a peasant to her. She complained to an old sage about her sad estate and how poor she was for the wealthy girl he'd sworn she was.

"I'm such a long way from home and who knows how long this trip will take? And who's seen it with their own eyes anyway? And this mission I'm assigned is too hard and most people don't care and others are surly and sometimes I'm sick and sometimes I'm sad. This can't be the way this is supposed to be. I'm a king's daughter, you say, but I do not live in his kingdom."

The eyes of the old sage sparkled beneath heavy lids. "Ah, but you will. And until then, his kingdom lives in you."

That once upon a time is now. That king's child is you. That hard job is yours. It's hard partly because, in a world adrift in darkness, bad news is easier to believe than good. In a sensory world, the seen is vastly easier to believe than the unseen, and yet "faith is the reality of what is hoped for, the proof of what is not seen" (Heb. 11:1). We are citizens of the kingdom of heaven arrested by grace and assigned mission in the clashing kingdoms of earth.

No small task but also no small adventure. The most riveting fiction literature can boast is a poor rival to our real story. We may wish Christ would make obvious to the mockers who we are and what we're doing on mission so we'd get more respect, but we'd hijack the glory along with the story. His ways are altogether different than ours. Out of His manifold wisdom God chose to reveal His Son and the work of His Spirit more often through whispers than shouts. But a day is coming when the skies will peel to the returning King and the earth will pound with bowing knees and the atmosphere will ring with confessing tongues declaring *Jesus is Lord*.

Matthew 13:24-52 is like a sketch pad of illustrations Jesus drew on an easel to offer His students glimpses into the artistry of the kingdom. Document each illustration below.

The kingdom of heaven is like ...

Offer three observations from the illustrations Jesus offered.

1.

2.

3.

This is the in-breaking of the kingdom of heaven where mystery is part of the artistry and hiddenness sweetens the knownness. In Dr. Russell Moore's words, "the kingdom of God is an invasion of an opposite and upside-down-minded kingdom into the existing realm of earth."[4]

The opening of John's third chapter stirs up images of a respectable Pharisee who could no longer fend off his fascination with Jesus of Nazareth, slinking out of his house in the black of night for a meet up. Few actions could have been less kosher to a religious sect feeling threatened by a small-town rabbi stealing their thunder. You can almost picture the man pulling his robe over his head, stealing furtive glances through the folds, making sure the coast was clear. Imagine him showing up at the door of the house where Jesus was staying, tapping on it surreptitiously and slipping through it the second it cracked open to the light of the world within. What you can know for certain about that clandestine encounter is found in permanent ink in John 3:1-21. As you read these words, appreciate the query between the seeker and the Teacher, and let it draw you in.

Record the question of Nicodemus in verse 4 in your own words.

Jesus responded to the Pharisee's question in John 3:5-6. That the night visitor couldn't wrap his imagination around Jesus' explanation is obvious from Christ's follow-up words in verse 7: "Do not be amazed that I told you that you must be born again." Jesus proceeded to compare the Spirit to the wind, but Nicodemus still couldn't grasp it.

Write the next question Nicodemus asked Jesus in John 3:9.

Does any part of today's discussion stir up a similar question? If so, express it to Him. If some of the concepts still seem too fictional to you, articulate to Jesus why you struggle to believe them.

Jesus' response to Nicodemus is paramount because it is the key that unlocks the door to eternal life. But give a surplus of attention to it today in specific reference to the kingdom of God. Glance one last time at John 3:5-6 and link it to Philippians 3:20 and Colossians 1:13. Jesus told Nicodemus how a mortal, a mere earthling, is suddenly born into the citizenship of heaven and, in the wording of Colossians 1:13, "rescued ... from the domain of darkness and transferred ... into the kingdom of the Son He loves." Write a succinct paraphrase of Christ's explanation in John 3:5-6.

This same means was your transfer into the kingdom of God and its transport into you. This was how your journey home began. You were born again, but this time by the Spirit and, this time, into royal blood. By this same means you will one day open your gorgeous regal eyes to the brilliance of life everlasting and find your feet standing on visible, touchable, royal real estate. You may not have felt a single miraculous thing when you were born a second time, yet it was the most riveting wonder of your earthly existence. How paradoxical that birth by natural means comes so dramatically, yet one can be born of the Spirit into the unconquerable kingdom of God without a whit of audible sound. To be sure, beyond your natural hearing, there was an outbreak of joy over your one individual life (Luke 15:7). You did not slip into the royal family unnoticed. You did not fade to gray in a crowd of others around the globe who placed their faith in Christ that same hour. You were planned, seen, known, regarded, chosen, and called by name. God knitted you together in your mother's womb and watched you draw your first gulp of air as she bore you into this world. He knew all along you'd be born a second time for another world where demons cannot play and darkness can't invade.

Express your gratitude to Him for the miracle of being born by the Holy Spirit into the royal family, recounting the circumstances around your conversion that are dearest to you now. Perhaps your rebirth came quietly from an earthly perspective. On the other hand, it may have come with dramatic awareness of being rescued from the savage jaws of death and destruction.

One final question remains for today. How is this kingdom reality woven into your daily mentality?

What peace it can bring to a deathbed and what consolation in deep suffering. But your best thoughts aren't meant to be saved for special occasions. Joy is most at risk in the routine. Right there in the wear and tear of your day-in, day-out existence—amid the dirty clothes, sinus infections, financial stresses, and family conflicts—knowing who you are, what you're doing here, and where you're headed changes everything.

"The Orthodox liturgy begins with the solemn doxology: 'Blessed is the Kingdom of the Father, the Son and the Holy Spirit, now and ever, and unto ages on ages.' From the beginning the destination is announced: the journey is to the Kingdom. This is where we are going—and not symbolically, but really. In the language of the Bible, which is *the* language of the Church, to bless the Kingdom is not simply to acclaim it. It is to declare it to be the goal, the end of all our desires and interests, of our whole life, the supreme and ultimate value of all that exists. To bless is to accept ... This acceptance is expressed in the solemn answer to the doxology: Amen."

ALEXANDER SCHMEMANN[5]

3.3

By the time I could sit cross-legged in front of a black and white TV, *The Wizard of Oz* was already iconic. According to the Library of Congress, "Because of its many television showings between 1956 and 1974, it has been seen by more viewers than any other movie."[6] The film both mesmerized and terrified me. I'd lay in bed that night after viewing the movie with the covers over my eyes, imagining a spinning farmhouse in a dark funnel cloud, a sky full of howling, winged monkeys, and a hideous green-faced witch with a crooked nose saying, "I'll get you, my pretty, and your little dog, too!"

The dog was an especially low blow.

To me, the worst part was Dorothy's horrible realization that there was no powerful wizard at all in Emerald City. Her hopes of finally getting home had been set on a weak, flustered, middle-aged man hiding behind a curtain. This disappointing reveal shook my faith a bit. My movieology and theology developed simultaneously because my father ran the local movie theater. I can recall sitting in Sunday School and church, wondering if, somewhere behind the veil, Jesus would turn out to be a myth made up by middle-aged men. The part I find most fascinating is that, even by the age of eight, I somehow knew the kingdom of God was no Oz and Jesus was no wizard. No matter how I entertained the parallels and the possibilities that Jesus could be nothing more than a man masquerading as God, I could not get myself sufficiently worked up to disbelieve. Though I was riddled by countless other childhood anxieties, I had an odd certainty about Jesus that I still can't explain. Something rang true about the man depicted in the watercolor pictures thumbtacked on the plaster walls of my Sunday School class. This conviction would carry me through a chronically unstable home life, childhood molestation, unhappily married parents, and a thousand disappointments. It would lead me back to repentance over and over in my titanic propensity to sin.

A few similarities and differences are striking enough for the movie classic to serve as a parable of sorts as we set our compass today. We are, in boldest biblical fact, on our way to a kingdom, but not in order to find our way home. It is our home. It lays not only in the distance. It is also near, living in us and expanding around us until we're residing safely and soundly within it. The biggest difference is the most important point of our compass today:

All the movies and novels depicting similar themes of harrowing adventures, impossible odds, and unlikely saviors are not over-dramatizations of our reality. In truth, they are not nearly dramatic enough. They can't be. We are wrapped up in a narrative no eye has fully seen, no ear has fully heard, and no human mind has ever conceived. In many ways these fictionalized stories, spun by the imaginations of mortals made in the image of God, are whispered hints and shifting shadows of the ineffable true one.

Look up each segment below for every element that heightens the drama and thickens the plot of the kingdom of heaven and its inhabitants on planet Earth. Record the elements under the categories you deem most fitting. Some may fit in more than one category. For example, if the segment conveys information about individuals involved in the kingdom drama, document it under "Characters." Check off each Scripture segment after you've read it and documented the information under at least one of the six categories.

Matthew 18:1-5
Matthew 21:28-32
Luke 22:24-30
1 Corinthians 4:20
1 Corinthians 15:24-27
Ephesians 6:11-13
Hebrews 12:26-29
Revelation 12:10-12

CHARACTERS:

CONFLICTS:

SPECIAL EFFECTS:

PLOT TWISTS:

CLIMACTIC POINTS:

OTHER:

The quotation of Paul's encouragement to the disciples in Acts 14:22 provides an unflinching summation for the harrowing adventure. Write it here:

The vision of the apostle John provides an astonishing culmination for the adventurers in Revelation 5:8-10. Read these three verses then write verse 10 here:

The "earth" the revelator references will be a brand spanking new one, by the way (Rev. 21:1). Glance over all you have documented. Try to think of a single movie to match the real, live storyline that is underway in the kingdom of God. If that's not drama, we don't know it when we see it. You're in the middle of it and so am I. So were all the saints before us and so will be all the ones who come after us. No wonder life gets so hard. Cosmic powers in this present darkness and spiritual forces of evil in the heavenly places are a far cry from a green-faced witch and flying monkeys. For all we know, a musical score could be playing beyond our hearing at the heights of our rescue. The psalmist said of God, "You … surround me with songs of deliverance" (Psalm 32:7, NIV).

You are not just part of a great story. You are part of *the* great story. A story so compelling that God begins it in Genesis with the words, "Let there be" (Gen. 1:3), and draws toward a close in Revelation with "it is done" (Rev. 21:6). Then starts all over again. Only this time, there will be no serpent in the garden.

No fall of man.

No sin or curse.

No sickness or death.

For the Lamb has overcome.

Today's query revolves around Acts 14:21-22 with the goal of allowing God Himself to strengthen and encourage you through His Word. Meditate on the segment and give it time to soak. Underline or circle any words or phrases that you find especially significant. Draw arrows from them to the margins and other blank spaces and jot down exhortations to yourself.

> After they had evangelized that town and made many disciples, they returned to Lystra, to Iconium, and to Antioch, strengthening the disciples by encouraging them to continue in the faith and by telling them, "*It is necessary to pass through many troubles on our way into the kingdom of God.*"
>
> **ACTS 14:21-22, HCSB (EMPHASIS MINE)**

Several definitions may add depth and particular meaning to the passage. The Greek term that translates *troubles* has a wide range of meanings, encompassing everything from feeling pressed and pressured to feeling utterly crushed or broken. It expresses "pressure from evils, affliction, distress" and can apply to a woman in the pangs of childbirth (John 16:21).[7]

The lexical word translated *strengthening* is *epistērízō* from *epí*, an intensive, and *stērízō, to strengthen, support*. Literally, *to place firmly upon*.[8] It captures the idea of leaning or resting upon something or someone for support. As a point of interest, you probably recognize the related word *steroid* in *stērízō*. An anabolic steroid is usually a synthetic hormone "used medically especially to promote tissue growth, and [is] sometimes abused by athletes to increase the size and strength of their muscles and improve endurance."[9] The kind of strength referenced in Acts 14:22

isn't synthetic. It's supernatural. It promotes growth in your faith, increases the size and strength of your spiritual muscle, and improves your soul's endurance in your arduous journey to the kingdom. Best of all, you can draw it from your all-powerful and compassionate God any time you need it without ever abusing it.

Read all of Isaiah 40. How many questions reside in this chapter in the translation you are using?

Reread each of the questions in Isaiah 40:12-14 and answer them to the best of your understanding in a brief prayer in this space.

Voice to God every detail that encourages you in Isaiah 40:1-11.

Note the similarities of care in the imagery used for God in Isaiah 40:11 and Christ in John 10:7-16. Recount to your Good Shepherd what He has done for His sheep.

Return to Isaiah 40 and record every question found in verses 25-31.

Are you tired, loved one of God? Weary or faint? If so, freely express to God why.

Profess to God everything He does according to Isaiah 40:25-31.

Conclude by boldly asking Him to do those things for you, to strengthen and encourage you. After all, through many tribulations, pressures, and stresses you journey home, mile by mile, to His glorious kingdom. Every inch will prove worth your trouble.

3.4

My own personal great awakening occurred in my mid-thirties. It was not a tender awakening like I often enacted with my sleeping daughters, sitting on the sides of their beds, rubbing their backs, pulling their long hair away from their ears and whispering, "Time to get up, my little sweeties. It's a school day. This is the day the Lord has made." Nope. It was like a siren blaring at deafening volume. And it didn't wake me up from a nightmare. It woke me up to a nightmare. Like you and each of our fellow Jesus followers, I had a divine calling, and I'd managed by God's grace to stumble into mine by then. Satan intended to stop me, but Jesus intended to sanctify and fortify me.

I'd never had an easy life so my baseline was no bed of roses. However, almost overnight I went from wrestling with my past and with my equally troubled husband and a tormented little boy who lived with us, to wrestling with dark forces the likes of which I didn't even know existed. I ran up against opposition, demonic seduction, and oppression I'd never before encountered. I'd come of age in my walk of faith, and that faith would be tested to the limits. I vividly recall asking anyone who'd listen, "Why didn't anybody tell me it would be like this?"

Has the same question ever come from your mouth? If so, what circumstances prompted it?

No doubt many pastors and teachers were equipping their listeners for the blistering heat of spiritual warfare and how to suffer well for Christ's name. However, I suspect the majority of American churches, including the five I'd attended in my lifetime, had tidier discipleship approaches. The nation I call home and dearly love was a safe place for most Christians, and belief in Christ was not only accepted, it was expected in many leadership positions, even in non-religious environments.

In churches like mine, our privilege increasingly altered our perception, and our perception increasingly altered our discipleship. The alteration was not intentionally misleading. It was the truth as many Christians in the prosperous West experienced it. I believe some of the prosperity gospel presently preached grew like wild shoots out of more innocent roots. Please understand, my parents never had an extra dime nor did Keith and I. But we were still among the nation's privileged in many ways. The churches of my younger years taught and preached segments of the New Testament describing the rigors of the early Jesus followers, but we viewed those primarily as marks of Christianity's sacrificial beginnings. Those were neither our experiences nor expectations.

Meanwhile, Christians were being persecuted, tortured, and murdered in disturbing numbers on the same globe. We'd hear about them occasionally, and accordingly react with horror, but we struggled to see how our lives connected with theirs. We couldn't fathom such atrocities happening to us. However, here we sit, you and I, in a public atmosphere increasingly hostile to the gospel. Some of those faraway cruelties are not quite as comfortably farfetched anymore.

We can be misled about the difficulties of following Christ by any number of sources, but from my vantage point, it seems the most common within a church context are these:

Ambitious shepherds only out for a big flock;

Greedy shepherds out to fleece the flock;

Sentimental shepherds keeping it sweet for the flock;

Misguided shepherds deluding the flock;

Untrained shepherds ill-equipping the flock.

None reflects the tenor of New Testament teaching. Since trust is crucial in any authentically intimate relationship, the following realization is monumental: if we've been misled, we have not been misled by Jesus. This truth in both its startling beauty and vulnerability was there all along in black and white. Today you'll center on the vulnerability of being a disciple of Jesus. Tomorrow you'll draw this week's quest to a close with the sheer beauty of it.

The tenth chapter of Matthew records the instructions Jesus gave His first disciples when He sent them out to proclaim the nearness of the kingdom of heaven. Some of His warnings involved prophecies that would reach ultimate fulfillment in later years as persecution broke out against the church after the outpouring of the Spirit. With pen in hand, read all the way through Matthew 10. List in the first column every detail that conveys the vulnerability of those first disciples.

VULNERABILITY	KIND OF VULNERABILITY

Go back to the list and, where possible, categorize what kind of vulnerability each description represents in the second column. For instance, was the vulnerability financial? Social? Familial? Physical? Were they placed at risk with governing authorities? You might categorize that example as "legal" vulnerability. Document your categories in the right hand column.

The full stretch of the New Testament canon remains consistent regarding the temporal vulnerability Jesus followers face in this world system. It is inhospitable to children of light. To be sure, intensities vary according to the environment, but no one who seeks to closely follow Jesus will be invulnerable in "this present darkness" (Eph. 6:12, ESV). "In fact, all who want to live a godly life in Christ Jesus will be persecuted" (2 Tim. 3:12).

We might argue that some environments on earth actually promote Christianity, and believers within these perimeters don't seem vulnerable at all. The scary thing is, the most favorable conditions can make us vulnerable to the most profound loss of all: the loss of our Christlikeness. Matthew 10:16 echoes the words of Jesus from age to age and shore to shore: "Look, I'm sending you out like sheep among wolves." Public environments favorable to Christianity demand vigilance on the part of Jesus followers against a seductive reversal: becoming wolves among sheep. When we live in safety, we have a tendency to lose focus. We turn from the mission and turn on each other. Jesus followers with an upper hand have an enormous responsibility to use their muscle to reach down as Jesus did. He wielded power primarily on behalf of the powerless and the overpowered. Imitating Jesus will always involve sacrificial love and attentiveness to the marginalized, despised, and sin-wrecked. It will always check our motives and call us to die to our selfish ambitions. Because these mind-sets are contrary both to our human nature and worldly culture, they won't come easy, but you and I aren't called to easy. We're called to the impossible.

Jesus held tightly to the tension of grace and truth, leaving neither slack. Holding similar tension will never cease to be a challenge for us. The temptation will ever be to hold onto one and let go of the other. Wisdom knows it is never invulnerable in this temporal realm. Any strong leader can become an oppressor and no oppressor is more likely to rationalize the use of improper force than one with religious zeal.

Just ask Saul of Tarsus. Take a fresh look at Acts 9:1-18 and note the dramatic shift from his bullying to his vulnerability. List every way his encounter with Christ ushered him into fresh vulnerability.

This is the kind of lesson a pastor could preach to a packed house if he intended to incite a stampede to the parking lot at the altar call. Or, is it? One of the chief reasons much is left unsaid in our churches about the cost of discipleship is our fear that people will run for their lives away from Jesus. We wonder, *who on earth would sign up for this?* So, why didn't the twelve hightail it the opposite direction after talk of floggings, betrayals, persecutions, and killings? And, likewise, the seventy-two in Luke 10 who were sent out by Jesus with similar instructions?

Because they found Someone worth everything. That same proud man who'd been struck blind by a flash of glory on the road to Damascus could not possibly have had more to lose in giving his life to Jesus. His whole identity was wrapped up in the stature he'd attained in Judaism. It was everything he'd wanted. Everything he'd worked for. Every relationship he had was within its construct. He was "a Hebrew born of Hebrews; regarding the law, a Pharisee ... regarding the righteousness that is in the law, blameless" (Phil. 3:5-6). Yet he wrote ...

> But everything that was a gain to me, I have considered to be a loss because of Christ. More than that, I also consider everything to be a loss in view of the surpassing value of knowing Christ Jesus my Lord. Because of him I have suffered the loss of all things and consider them filth, so that I may gain Christ.
>
> **PHILIPPIANS 3:7-8**

I'm utterly convinced we're all looking for Someone worth absolutely everything. The search was on the moment we emerged in birth and the pupils of our eyes dilated in the light. The search is inextricably strung into our DNA. We're all looking for someone big enough, beautiful enough, bold enough, brilliant enough, brave enough, otherworldly enough, someone finally good enough to rescue us from our self-obsession and sweep us up into a love worth dying for. The sublime irony is that, right there in that self-crucifying love, we finally come alive.

Inscribe the words of God in Psalm 49:15 in this space and take them personally.

Read Hebrews 6:10 and journal to God what you can be assured is true according to this verse.

Take in Mark 10:23-31. Record Christ's words in verses 29-31.

If anything He said in the previous segment is hard for you to understand, express it to Him. Part of your present quest is practicing dialogue with Him in the pages of Scripture by telling Him what His words mean to you, how they land on your heart, convict, compel, or even confuse you.

Lastly, read Mark 10:32-52. As you can see, Jesus and His disciples were walking together on a journey to Jerusalem. It would be Christ's final pilgrimage before His appointment with death on the cross. They would traverse through several villages before they arrived at their destination. The contrasting moments Mark documented in the verses you just read are like a walking, talking version of whiplash. Jesus knew exactly what was going to happen to Him at the end of this trip. He had, in fact, just stated to the twelve in startling terms what suffering and humiliation awaited Him. Imagine the kinds of horrors on His mind when James and John approached Him with their request for honor.

Remarkably, and surely not coincidentally, Jesus asked the same question in the subsequent scenes: first in verse 36 to the sons of Zebedee and then to the blind beggar in verse 51. Record the question here.

What you want Jesus to do for you matters to Him even if He challenges it or corrects skewed thinking. You know He can do anything. You know all authority has been given to Him. You know He loves you completely and unconditionally. You know He took that road to Jerusalem as surely for you as He did for those very first followers. He knows your heart intimately. He knows your fears and your dreams. Take a moment and reflect on today's quest. Spend the remainder of your journaling today answering the same question He brought to James and John and Bartimaeus.

3.5

The compass was set in our previous lesson on the temporal vulnerability Jesus told His followers they could expect from being His disciples. Today the point of the compass will take aim at the beauty of following Him. You saw glimpses of it strewn and sewn into the same commissioning in Matthew 10 where Christ warned His disciples of floggings and killings. Life is a mingling of vulnerability and beauty for the Jesus follower this side of seeing His glorious face. I have no wish to romanticize pain or minimize the cost of suffering, but I have to believe the beauty is not just in spite of the vulnerability but, in some significant measure, because of it. When all is said and done, it will not just be that you believed, served, loved, testified, gave, sacrificed, rejoiced, endured, hoped, and forgave.

It will be that you believed anyway.

Served anyway.

Loved Him anyway.

Testified anyway.

Gave anyway.

Sacrificed anyway.

Rejoiced anyway.

Endured anyway.

Hoped anyway.

Forgave those who harmed you anyway.

All while the flames of hell licked and blistered the soles of your tender feet. Don't think that won't matter. Your primary text today will be Luke 10:1-24, but you will go back and forth between the accounts of Luke and Matthew several times.

You will notice the similarities almost immediately, but also keep your eyes open for variances. Luke 10:1 and Matthew 10:1 highlight two different audiences. Record them here.

After you read Luke 10:1-24, go to Matthew 10 and peruse both chapters for every ray of beauty you see shining between the clouds of vulnerability in those passages. Record them below. I've given you one example.

MATTHEW 10	LUKE 10:1-24
Gave them His authority (v. 1)	

Return to Luke 10:1. How did Jesus send out the seventy-two?

Compare Matthew 10:1-4 and give attention to the way the Gospel writer paired the names of Christ's disciples. List each pair.

Mark's parallel account tells us Jesus "summoned the Twelve and began to send them out in pairs" (Mark 6:7). We don't have to be math wizards to calculate that Jesus could have covered twice the ground if He'd sent each of them out alone. He didn't. Think about it and offer five reasons why you think two were better than one.

1.

2.

3.

4.

5.

I wish I could sit across a table for two and hear your five reasons. These are the kinds of things I'd like to toss around in a conversation over a shared basket of sizzling, salty French fries. Discipleship involves a constant volleying between being apart and being a part. To pursue deeply satisfying intimacy with Christ, learning how to be apart from everyone else and alone with Him is a necessity. The old saying still has merit: who I am when no one's around is the real me. But discipleship also places a high premium on community and fellowship, on camaraderie and co-working. To know only how to be apart with Jesus but not a part of a holy partnership of believers leaves more than a deficit of human company. As paradoxical as this seems, it also subtracts from our knowledge of Christ. We are hard pressed to fully come to know Him in isolation from fellow Jesus followers even if we spend every waking moment in the Scriptures. Similarly, we are vastly less equipped in our callings and effective in our giftings if we're perpetual spiritual shut-ins, even if we're shut in our closets praying. Isolation is not His way. We are the body of Christ and all amputated appendages eventually dry up and die if they aren't willing to somehow reattach. If your physical health has you homebound, be bold and reach out to a local community of believers and find creative ways to co-serve.

When times are tough and you're about to give up, your fellow sojourners tell you to keep going. When you feel unwelcomed and unsuccessful, somebody's next to you, shaking the same dust off his road-weary feet. When you don't have a dime, you still have a friend. When you don't have the faith to get back on the path, someone can help you up with a handful of hers. When you get to glimpse a miracle, you have someone at hand to bear happy witness and, years later, to remind you it was real. A fellow believer who can make you laugh helps you bear your seasons of tears. We are sheep (plural) among wolves. You're not meant to pasture as one lone lamb surrounded by a howling pack. We need fellow sheep nearby who can bleat, "Remember, He said there'd be days like this." One common cause of loneliness is the natural human tendency to limit our search for comrades to people who look or seem very much like us. We will miss what would have surely been some of our favorite people on earth if we won't look beyond our mirror image in age, marital status, background, and personality.

If you have a comrade in the faith very different from you, describe the individual here and what riches he or she brings to your life.

As you listed rays of beauty amid the vulnerabilities, you probably caught the part in Luke 10 where Jesus said to His disciples, "whoever rejects you rejects me" (v. 16). Somehow we don't have to take rejection nearly so personally if someone bigger is taking it personally for us. But isn't the best part, hands down, the scene where the seventy-two returned in Luke 10:17-24? Behold the unbridled joy.

How many times do you find some form of the word *joy* in verses 17-21?

What caused the seventy-two such joy according to verse 17?

What caused Jesus His own particular joy according to verse 21?

We could drain a cartridge of ink with a detailed exposition of Luke 10:17-21 and savor every syllable of it. But, sticking with our space and goal, we could also perhaps fold that broad scroll small enough to slip it into a nutshell and say this: *it worked*. If you'll permit me the creative license, I'll explain by wrapping a little more language around those two words, assuming Christ's original followers were anything like us.

Jesus, that power You supplied us through that authority You lent us in Your name worked! And it worked through us: flawed flesh and blood, prone to wander, drawn to failure, and more often scared of our own shadows than emboldened by faith. Your power worked through us! YOU worked through us and from a distance, no less, sight unseen. It happened just like You said it would.

Of course Jesus knew it would, but isn't that part of the breathtaking joy of it? His foreknowledge did not extinguish His joy. Revisit Christ's enthralling response in Luke 10:18. One challenge of Bible interpretation is determining which time zone may be indicated: present, past, or future? God says of Himself, "I am … the one who is, who was, and who is to come" (Rev. 1:8). Time is His employee, not His boss. One statement could apply to all three—present, past, and future. This could well be the case regarding Luke 10:18. At the very least it had both present and future applications. According to Dr. J. B. Green, "The decisive fall of Satan is anticipated in the future, but it is already becoming manifest through the mission of Jesus and, by extension, through the ministry of his envoys."[10]

Lock your focus on Luke 10:21. See the word *rejoiced* or the NIV phrase *full of joy* in reference to Jesus? The Greek from which both are translated is a form of the word "***agalliáō*** … from ***ágan***, much, and ***hállomai***, to leap. To exult, leap for joy, to show one's joy by leaping and skipping denoting excessive or ecstatic joy and delight. Hence in the NT to rejoice, exult. Often spoken of rejoicing with song and dance."[11] ***Agalliáō*** is an inlet of joy filling and spilling into an outlet of expression. It's a volcanic eruption of the lava of joy. For Jesus it took the form of a praise break which I can only hope included a leap or two. The sequence in Luke 10:21-23 suggests He looked away from the seventy-two toward His Father to express worship for the wonder of His ways then turned back toward His disciples and told them how blessed they were.

We can assume the seventy-two ran into problems, or Jesus would have saved His breath on the predictions. Notice the seventy-two didn't talk nonstop about all that had gone wrong. Not one word was said about how the McGruffs over in Bethsaida had mistreated them or how the Wippleworths in Capernaum wouldn't let them in the house. They'd shaken whatever dust off their feet then and there. Appreciate the active ingredient in the name-brand prescription Jesus gave His followers for times they were unwelcomed, rejected, or withheld peace (Matt. 10:14; Luke 10:11). Jesus knows how powerless rejection makes a person feel. He provided those early followers with a perfect outlet, a physical demonstration of an internal resolve: "Shake the dust off your feet" (Matt.10:14).

Think of the directive conceptually as well as literally. Expound on what you believe it means and what good it does.

To be given authorization to shake off rejection and disesteem is no small thing. It helps rescue the servant of Christ from a victim mentality. I get to choose whether or not this rejection accompanies me down the road. I refuse it the right to cling to my feet and affect how I walk. Rejection will not be my co-traveler. I'm leaving it right where I found it.

According to Luke 10:17, the seventy-two had one thing on their minds to tell Jesus when they got back: powers greater than them had submitted to them because they operated under the authority of the greatest name ever proclaimed by tongues of mortal men.

Record Christ's words in Luke 10:18 and let them reverberate.

Satan depicted in heaven in this context may hint toward his role of accuser. *Devil*, his other common name, means *false accuser*.[12] Revelation 12:10 characterizes the devil as "the accuser of the brothers and sisters, who accuses them before our God day and night." He does not make accusations about you only in regard to your past. He also makes accusations regarding your future. His assaults on Job's character in Job 1:11 were predictive. He claimed Job would curse God to His face under adverse conditions. The devil could be voraciously accusing you of future unfaithfulness. By the power of Jesus' name, expose your accuser as the liar he's always been. When you endure to the end of a divine assignment, having yielded to Christ's authority and wielded His power against turmoil, tribulation, and untold satanic opposition, you are in prime condition for Jesus to speak those same words over you. You may be bruised. You may have scars. But, you—mere flesh and blood—have overcome and have given Jesus reason to erupt with joy. Satan placed a bet against you and lost.

Ask God to bring to your remembrance a time when Satan was overcome or thrown down, so to speak, where you were concerned. Recount it back to Jesus.

Maybe your journey's been too brief or turbulent to have that testimony. Maybe your present season is the perfect time to make a liar out of your accuser. If you are presently undergoing a fierce season and yearn for your present assignment to end in Christ's great joy, pray toward that end.

If you are lonely and lack fellow sojourners and partners in the faith, earnestly request them here and date your prayer to increase your praise when He answers. Ask Him to empower you to be obedient in cooperation with the process.

Return to Luke 10:20, and record Christ's redirection to the seventy-two toward the highest cause for praise.

Let that sink in. Believer, your name is written in heaven. Respond with praise to conclude today's query.

Take a moment and reflect on your quest so far. Look back over each day of study and journal a brief note about what spoke to you, what you learned, and what course corrections you need to make. Then, spend a moment in prayer, writing from your heart to the Lord as you move forward on this quest.

DAY 1

Truths I encountered:

What I learned about myself and Jesus:

Course corrections I need to make:

DAY 2

Truths I encountered:

What I learned about myself and Jesus:

Course corrections I need to make:

DAY 3

Truths I encountered:

What I learned about myself and Jesus:

Course corrections I need to make:

DAY 4

Truths I encountered:

What I learned about myself and Jesus:

Course corrections I need to make:

DAY 5

Truths I encountered:

What I learned about myself and Jesus:

Course corrections I need to make:

Lord, as I move forward ...

Four

Video and audio sessions available for purchase at LifeWay.com/TheQuest.

#QuestStudy

4.1

Since Week Five is the final stretch of our quest and we Christ followers are under the new covenant, our map will navigate us next week almost exclusively through New Testament passages. Our present week, however, will steer us to different stops on the Old Testament atlas where questions hold particular prominence. Even in the embryonic stage of planning this curriculum, I knew the Scripture segments we have ahead of us this week were absolute essentials to get a solid grasp of our concept.

In Week One, Day Three, Christ's intriguing greeting to Nathanael upon their first encounter (John 1:47) called for an explanation that involved a brief mention of the patriarch Jacob. I promised you at that time we'd circle back to him. Today sends us to that cul-de-sac.

Revisit John 1:47-51 and record what Christ said to Nathanael in verse 47.

Christ's play on words drew a vivid contrast between Nathanael and his ancestor, Jacob, whose scheming deceit was a notorious part of Israel's narrative. Jacob, the grandson of Abraham and the younger of Isaac's twin sons, exploited his brother's exhaustion by goading him into selling his birthright for a pot of stew (Gen. 25:29-34). Later Jacob tricked his old, weak-eyed father into giving him the blessing of the firstborn that his father thought he was giving to Esau. In doing so, Isaac gave the younger lordship over the older (Gen. 27). Jacob, who'd come into the world grasping Esau's heel, finally managed in adulthood to yank hard enough to entirely supplant him. Jacob successfully fooled both brother and father, but no manipulation or masquerade is clever enough to cloud the eyes of God. He'd pry that deception loose from the stony heart of Jacob with painstaking patience.

Read Genesis 27:41-45 and record what happened.

Reflect on the line, "Listen, your brother Esau is consoling himself by planning to kill you." We all console ourselves in one way or another when things go wrong, especially when we feel overlooked, rejected, or cheated. Perhaps no other indicator gives a more accurate reading of our heart condition than how we console ourselves. This makes the subject of self-comfort worth squirming over. I won't ask you to fill in the following blank on paper, but please do so in your thoughts while I do the same.

"[Your name] is consoling herself/himself by________________________."

Our consolations over the wrongs done to us can turn out to be more destructive than the wrongs themselves. In our final week we'll collect healthy consolations.

Jacob's fraudulence may have bought him the blessing, but it bounced him far from the home he loved and from the company of his aging father. He traveled as far as sunlight would let him. Then he stopped for the night, made a pillow of stone, and had a peculiar dream.

Read Genesis 28:10-22 and describe it.

How it is linked to John 1:47-51?

God's stairway revelation to Jacob through the dream presents us with several options: God either overflows with inconceivable grace and faithfulness, or He doesn't have a problem with His people lying and conniving to get what they want. When a hammer of chastisement doesn't come down quickly, we're tempted to conclude God was unoffended by wrongdoing. However, thankfully, He appears to prefer a chisel over a sledgehammer. He chips away at our rough and jagged edges with painstaking patience.

The divine Carpenter is also the Great Physician, and sometimes He treats our sickness with a long, bitter taste of our own medicine. Jacob ran from Esau straight into the hands of Laban whose trickery, deception, and manipulation held him hostage for two solid decades. Still, God prospered Jacob. But, as God's favor increased, Laban's favor decreased. Just when things were about to go from bad to ugly, Jacob received word from the Lord.

What did God tell Jacob to do in Genesis 31:3?

After no small drama with Laban, Jacob and his expansive family, his servants, and his flocks and herds were on their way. There was just one obstacle: they had to trek through Esau's land to get back home. Isn't that often how the faith journey goes? We have to face our biggest messes and worst fears on the road to the fulfillment of God's promises to us.

If this reminds you of a specific part of your own journey with God, express how.

As Genesis 32 unfolds, over twenty years have blown off the calendar since Jacob and Esau were last together. Time heals all wounds, the saying goes, but most of us know better. Time can as easily expose, infect, and spread wounds. Time sometimes heals, but it always tells.

Read Genesis 32:1-23. In these twenty-three verses you can find vestiges of the old scheming Jacob and hints of a nascent man of faith. Categorize each under the proper heading.

SIGNS OF THE OLD JACOB	HINTS OF A NEW JACOB

The wrestling match within Jacob paled in comparison to the most mysterious wrestling match between two figures in the wide span of Scripture.

Read Genesis 32:24-32. List elements that make the scene particularly enigmatic.

Jacob wasn't just on his way home. He was on his way to honesty. He'd just fought his first honest fight. How does Hosea 12:3-4 add some volume to the scene with a few additional descriptions?

All the angel did to end the fight was strike Jacob's hip socket to dislocate the joint; therefore, the moral of the story was not Jacob's superior might. Indeed his own summation of the fight was that he'd "seen God face to face," yet his life had "been spared" (v. 30). He never doubted he was at the enigmatic wrestler's mercy. The game-changer for Jacob was that he refused to quit.

"I will not let you go unless ________________________________!"

GENESIS 32:26b

That, Beloved, is faith. Faith knows that, when you wrestle with God, if you'll hang on long enough, the blessing will come. Sometimes we just let go too soon.

Jacob had come by his father Isaac's blessing dishonestly. He did not intend to come by this one the same way. First, God required the patriarch to own up to his lifelong bent toward the sin.

What question did the angel ask in Genesis 32:27?

God wasn't asking for his driver's license. He was after his confession. Write some of the meanings of the name Jacob to complete this sentence (Gen. 27:35-36).

My name is ...

Knowing God sees straight through every fleck of pretense and false bravado serves as a guardian to our souls, especially in a culture where image is supreme. If we could fool God with external appearances, the toxic slush in our interior life would go virtually unchecked until it suddenly gushed out in a muddy blitz. Vanity would make us fools and paupers. Insatiable egos would make us insufferable. Territorialism would make rivals out of friends. Simmering resentment would make us vindictive, and lust would enslave us to sexual addiction. He'll call it out before it gushes out if we'll listen and let go.

In Genesis 32:28 the angel did something Jacob needed more than anything but couldn't have known to ask. What was it?

The new name mimicked the sound of the Hebrew phrase "he struggled (with) God."[1] Genesis 32:31 paints a breathtaking portrait in the stroke of a single verse. Picture the sunrise on the dew-sparkling landscape of a place called Penuel, meaning *face of God*. Lean forward into that rising sun and you'll see the silhouette of a limping man all by himself entering into his future having come to terms with his past. He still had an old problem to face but the old problem no longer had the same old person.

Write the question in Genesis 32:27 once again, but this time let it be addressed to you.

Even though God is well acquainted with your name, blood type, cell structure, personality profile, and every other detail of your life including the precise number of hairs on your head, write out your full name. If your name has any special meaning or significance to you, tell it to God. Also tell Him if you dislike it and why.

Names aren't the only way people identify one another; they also use labels. Perhaps you've been derogatorily labeled. If so, name those labels to God, and describe to Him their negative impact.

Many labels are prejudicial and without basis. If, on the other hand, you feel like you helped invite a derogatory label with your mistakes or sin, own your part of the responsibility before your gracious and merciful God if you haven't already done so. Ask Him today to peel off those labels and to strip them henceforth of any adhesive power to stick to you.

In this segment, willingly wrestle in prayer over any similarities you may have to Jacob. Duplicity with man clogs intimacy with God. Every human heart is prone to deceive and be deceived. It may be through subtler means like flattery, manipulation, and false bravado, or it may be through audaciously public means like false claims, testimonies, and identities. Regardless of which means best describes you, the temptation to deceive is as predictable as your next heartbeat. Since the goal of this excursion is intimacy with God, talk to Him openly about any Jacob-like tendencies in your heart, and ask Him to root them out. Your true self, scars and all, is beautiful. If you have a limp, don't hide it. It may be the very thing that keeps you walking closely with God.

Your final reading is Genesis 33:1-4. Refreshing, isn't it? Use this space to thank God for allowing some situations to turn out far differently than you feared. If an encounter or confrontation on the horizon is causing you considerable dread, make your petition for a different ending than you're prone to expect.

Would you like to know something wonderful? There may be a bit of wordplay in the Jacob narrative in regard to the word *wrestled* in Genesis 32:24 and *embraced* in Genesis 33:4 (ESV). In Hebrew, the spelling for *wrestle* (*abaq*) and *embrace* (*habaq*) differ by only one letter, and their pronunciations provide a sublime rhyme.[2]

Mystery is inherent in a long journey with God. When you're tempted to turn away from Him over unanswered questions, turn toward Him instead and struggle honestly. Wrestling with God can be its own form of intimacy. It's face-to-face and hands on. And remember, if you'll hang on long enough, the blessing will come and that wrestling match will turn into embrace.

4.2

I love where our compass is pointing us today. We have such a rich history of faith spanning thousands of years. Your reading today surrounds two of the most significant Old Testament events in the history of God's people. Read each segment and supply the information requested. Peruse surrounding chapters for context if needed.

EXODUS 12:1-28

What event does this segment describe?

Where did it take place?

How were they told to memorialize it?

Write out the verse containing the one question asked in this portion of Scripture.

JOSHUA 4

What event does this segment describe?

Where did it take place?

How were they told to memorialize it?

Write out the two verses that contain questions in this portion of Scripture.

Circle the word "when" in each of the verses you wrote in the assignment on the previous page. Why do you suppose the verses didn't use the word "if" instead?

In Rabbi Ted Falcon's book *Judaism for Dummies*, he writes, "Although the idea of a complete surrender to faith, a surrender to God, is harmonious with many Christian and Muslim beliefs, it's much less comfortable for most Jews, who are traditionally taught to question in order to learn more deeply. Judaism tends to encourage individuals to explore their own personal relationship with God. For people who are comfortable with the idea of surrender, God-wrestling is not an easy concept."[3]

Certainly Christians are called to a life surrendered to Christ, but surrender does not preclude questions. After all, no one could have been more surrendered to His Father's will than Jesus on the cross, yet, nailed to that very tree, He cried out one of the most piercing questions ever to erupt from the heart of a man. More on that next week. Falcon's insight into Judaism, however, is compelling in our present quest, particularly because Christianity cannot be clipped from its Jewish roots without cutting off its Head. Jesus is Jewish. When we come by faith into Christ, Gentiles do not become Jewish, but we do become spiritual descendants of His ancestral line.

Surrender does not preclude *questions*.

Jot Galatians 3:29 here.

In ancient Judaism, questions were not squiggly roads to be avoided in the walk of faith. Rather, they were adventures to be taken, where one leans into the learning curves of discussion, deliberation, and healthy debate. Questions were means of discovery, exposing what was both known and not yet known. They were not surfaced proofs of doubt or detours of the weak but often quite the opposite. A true quest requires boots and swords to hack through the thorns and briars to get to the blooms without bleeding.

Christ's penchant for engaging His audience and baffling His critics through Q&A in His three-year ministry is easily verifiable in the Gospels. What you may find delightful is the proof that it wasn't a recent development for Him or inconsistent with the rabbinic approaches of His day. Generous amounts of ink were given to Jesus' infancy and adulthood in Scripture, but we're offered one small glimpse of Christ's boyhood.

Read Luke 2:41-50. How old was Jesus? Where was He and what exactly was He doing?

What does verse 47 convey?

The classroom was rarely just class in ancient rabbinic Judaism. Class was quest. Learning was adventure. I can't think of a better way to study the Bible.

Reflect on your reading in Exodus 12 and Joshua 4 and revisit your notation of the verses including the phrase "when your children ask." When—not if—makes perfect sense to parents because a typical child's questions know no end. This is especially true on a road trip when, worn to a nub, we finally resort to our last defense: "Now, let's play the quiet game. The last one to talk wins." By God's glorious design, children are hardwired to inquire. The two occasions in Joshua 4 are inquiries Scripture anticipates about the meaning of the stones taken from the middle of the Jordan as the people of God crossed over to their promised land. Rewind further in time to Exodus 12:26 in the context of Passover.

"When your children ask you, 'What does this ceremony mean to you?'"

This single question shaped the tradition still widely practiced in Passover meal observances. The entire Exodus narrative is retold in answer to a designated child at the supper table (the youngest who is old enough to participate) asking specific questions with one theme: "Why is this night different than all other nights?"[4]

Nothing swings a door wide open like a question. The New Testament also anticipates numerous questions, but these are posed to believers in Christ. First Peter 3:15 anticipates one of the most powerful.

Rewrite the question in your own words.

In a world draining hope like water from an unplugged tub, all it takes to attract curiosity is to offer a small cup sloshing with it. Most of our lives are graced by human hopes that are tonic to the soul like a newborn in the family or a promising job opportunity or a guy who might be the one or glimpses of flames among what you thought were dying embers. These are gifts from God—common graces—to be savored with thanksgiving. But only one hope floats when despair drags all others to the bottom.

Your life in Christ tells a great story. What is it? Can you articulate it? Do people ever ask you about it? You may wish you had a story less dramatic or more breathtaking, but you have something better: you have your own. Today's query will direct your prayers toward commemorating significant chapters in your story and penning them through a fresh lens.

The two occasions in Scripture containing the instruction "when your children ask" represent two types of divine deliverance. In Exodus 12, God delivered the Israelites from their wicked, enslaving taskmaster. In Joshua 4, God delivered the Israelites to their promised land.

In Exodus 12, God delivered them *from*.

In Joshua 4, God delivered them *to*.

Deuteronomy 6:20-25 displays the juxtaposition perfectly. Read the segment, noting the same anticipation of the younger generations' questions. Then write Deuteronomy 6:23 in this space: Why did God bring them out?

Your story over time is also meant to display both elements—how God brought you out to bring you in—for the splendor of God's glory. If you are in Christ, you've experienced your own Passover in its truest fulfillment through your salvation. But deliverance from the dominion of the devil was not all Christ came to offer you. When God delivers you out of something, He's not finished. He has something good and profitable He wants to deliver you to. Think of your own promised land as places where you experience fulfilled promises of God. To the best of your understanding, you're where God wants you for now and your life is bearing fruit. Difficulties still abound, of course, but the spiritual ground God has given you is fertile. You sow the seeds of His Word—sometimes with joy, sometimes with tears, but always with faith—and sooner or later tender green shoots sprout from the ground. Sometimes that soil either dries up permanently, or the harvest becomes self-sufficient. At that point, God may move you to another field to plant further seed and bear further fruit. Don't assume failure in the former unless God convicts you of sin or disobedience. Assume transfer. A lot of ground needs covering to spread the kingdom.

Think first in terms of the Passover metaphor in your story: when God delivered you from or brought you out.

Read 1 Corinthians 5:7, and then profess to Christ who He is to you by the reference made to Him in this verse.

Read 1 Peter 1:14-21, and recount to Jesus what the passage conveys He has done for you.

Case those same eight verses in 1 Peter as God's words to you regarding what He asks of those redeemed by His Son's precious blood. List His requests here.

Pull yourself up to your own Passover table where Christ is your Passover Lamb and observe a moment of deliberate remembrance. Reflect on when your journey of faith really began. Remember, in Passover celebrations, the questions of the children all pointed to one primary inquiry: "Why is this night different than all other nights?" When you came to truly believe what Jesus had done for you and received His gift of grace through the outpouring of His blood, what about that particular season of your life made you ripe for faith? In tweaked wording of the children's question, why was that time different than all the other times? If your memories of that time have faded somewhat, ask God to remind you. Did He use circumstances or people as instruments to help draw you? Or what finally convinced you? Maybe the following wording might steer your pen best: Why was this Savior different than all the world's offerings of false saviors? Speak directly to God in your response.

The Lord's Supper is the closest official ceremony New Testament believers observe to the Jewish Passover meal. Christ instituted it by no mere coincidence at the Passover table with His disciples on the evening before His death. Fathom that He who sat at the head of the Passover table was also its Lamb.

Read 1 Corinthians 11:23-26. Borrowing the wording of Exodus 12:26, "What does this ceremony mean to you?"

Hopefully you've had the opportunity to observe the Lord's Supper with a body of believers numerous times. What does it mean to you? Again, direct your response straight to Jesus.

Has there been a time you took the cup and the bread in remembrance of Christ when it had particular significance to you? Recall it to Christ.

Reflect on your own version of Joshua 4. If you've accrued enough miles on your journey with Jesus, you have memories with Him of a tremendously significant passage of time where He escorted you to a new place of living out your faith. If it was anything like the original crossing of the Jordan, that time of your life was both frightening and full of wonder. Think back on it and pull out some memory stones: people, events, and moments you never want to forget. Note several of them below. In the wording of Joshua 4:6, what do these stones mean to you? Direct your response to the God who made a way for you.

Your adventure is not over by a long shot. Let God have the last word today.

Write Isaiah 43:19 in this space. Don't force it to apply to your immediate season, but if it does, be more afraid of missing the next adventure with Him than of taking it. You've got rivers yet to cross and memory stones yet to collect. Face forward. Move out.

4.3

I wish I could ask you face-to-face if this journey is doing anything for you. It's been deeply meaningful to me to see biblical grounds for grappling as part of growing, mystery as part of intimacy, and to realize that without questions there is no quest. We're not wind-up toys God built for His Son to play with, walking mindless and stiff-legged across a flat earth till we fall off the edge and He catches us and cackles, "Gotcha!"

Keep an ear to the world, and you'll hear conclusions drawn that the Bible defies:

There is no God at all.

There may be a God, but, if so, He's no different than Dr. Frankenstein, at the mercy of the monsters He created.

If there is a God, He has either checked out on planet Earth, or He's cruel and spiteful.

If there is a compassionate God, He is clearly not all powerful.

If there is an all-powerful God, He is clearly not compassionate.

If there is an attentive God, He plays favorites.

There is probably a God, but there's no knowing Him and certainly no trusting Him.

At some particularly horrifying moments, have you seriously entertained any of those thoughts? If your honest answer is no, my hat is off to you. If your answer is yes, that makes two of us. What were the conditions and which one(s) of those options seemed the most viable?

This is where I mostly land when the suffering, injustice, and evil in this world hammers me or touches my loved ones: *The thing of it is, God, I know good and well You are all powerful, all glorious, all knowing, all present, all seeing, all loving, all holy, always good, always compassionate, always in control, always on Your throne, always righteous, unutterably light, and in You is no darkness at all. I know for a biblical fact You are at the same time both just and merciful. In You is both truth and grace. You are well able to heal and well able to sustain and comfort when You don't. I know these things, Lord! I know them to my bones. But why did this happen? Why didn't You intervene? Why do You wait?*

With an earnest heart and respect for His sovereignty and supremacy, I think those kinds of questions are welcomed. They are not questioning His character. They are cries of a finite lover of Jesus begging to understand His higher ways. Perhaps like you, I even already know some of the grown-up answers to the very *why* and *how could You* questions that sometimes erupt from my mouth between sobs. But asking them keeps me talking to Him instead of turning away from Him when I'm beside myself with grief or horror. I'm not sure how this will go over with you, but sometimes, when the devastation is personal, I've said to Him in a rivers of tears, "God, this hurts my feelings!"

Those moments seem like legitimate intimacy with God to me. I recall the day my oldest daughter called me in horror and told me a high school friend of hers and her one-year-old baby had been killed in a car accident. What made the tragedy most unfathomable was that her friend's parents had only recently buried her older sister. I went straight to the floor and cried until I thought my ribs would break, asking *why? how? what on earth?* and every other question roaring in my soul. Each time I've landed in that brutal state of mind, His comfort would eventually come to ease the straining chasm of unanswered questions. Once again, God would use His Word and the witness of His Spirit to reassure me of His unfailing, unchanging attributes. I'd ask *why*. He'd answer *who*.

Quickly cover the next paragraph with your hand and keep it there until I pose a question and you take a shot at answering it. Ready? On the opening day of our study, I shared with you that, according to J. L. Hancock's research in his book *All the Questions in the Bible*, the KJV is home to 3,298 questions.[5] In the book, he also breaks the number of questions down according to books of the Bible. Three guesses which book of the Bible contains the most questions. If you have some familiarity with the Scriptures, offer your guesses.

Need a hint? It's in the Old Testament.

Time's up. If you guessed the book between Esther and Psalms, you get an A+ on today's pop quiz. The Book of Job wins by a landslide with an astonishing tally of 329. Its closest Old Testament contenders are Jeremiah (195), Isaiah (190), Psalms (163), 1 Samuel (157), and Genesis (149). The New Testament opens strong with Matthew at 177, Mark at 121, Luke at 165, and John at 167.

You can show off your mad math skills by calculating the total number of questions in the four Gospels: _______.

The frequency of questions in the Gospels strongly supports a primary point in this quest: inquiry was stylistic to Christ's approach. He asked questions, answered questions, and caused questions.

It's a good thing Jesus wasn't opposed to questions, or the Book of Job might not have rolled onto the holy scroll. Most theologians agree the overarching question marking the Book of Job is "Why do the righteous suffer?" We ask the same question today alongside "Why do the innocent suffer?" What makes this theme particularly telling is that Job may well be one of the oldest books in the entire Bible. If it is not among the oldest, its setting certainly is: "Job apparently lived in the patriarchal or prepatriarchal days, for not only does he not mention the Law or the exodus, but he is pictured as a wealthy nomad (Job 1:3; 42:12) who is still offering sacrifices himself (Job 1:5; 42:8)."[6]

Appreciate what can be surmised from the dating: ours is not a God who dodges questions or dwells in lofty denial of the sufferings and grapplings of the very humanity He created. He weaved the themes in His own Word by His own wisdom. You have to respect a God so confident in His goodness, righteousness, blamelessness, and integrity that His reputation isn't an ounce threatened by the dialogue in this jaw-dropping book. On the contrary, including it was His idea.

Flip through the entire Book of Job and note how the first two chapters and most of the final chapter appear on the page in contrast to the rest of the book. Assuming your translation shows a variance, what difference do you see?

Job 1, 2, and 42:7-17 are written in prose. The thirty-nine chapters in between are poetry with the brief exceptions of the introductions of speakers. Our compass for today and tomorrow will be set on this book. Please don't be intimidated or filled with dread. Be thankful God openly invites us into this discussion on the sacred page. We don't have to talk behind His back. Take these two lessons on bravely because no honest quest can detour around the kinds of questions we'll encounter. Also keep in mind that Job's story stands out precisely because the depth of his suffering was exceptional. Suffering and loss of this magnitude do tragically occur in countries where famine or war rages. May God have mercy and keep our eyes open with compassion, our mouths open with prayer, and our wallets open with giving to help alleviate this suffering. But to fear that we could jinx ourselves into severe suffering by reading Job is superstitious and faithless. Let's not stoop to that. Satan continually leverages our worst fears for his best threats. Bring them to Jesus. He is well acquainted with our vulnerability and triumphs victoriously over our enemy through the power of His cross. One day the devil will pay. Until then, never forget that Jesus, your advocate, ascended to the heavens and sat down at the right hand of God. Read Hebrews 7:25 below. (Sometimes only the KJV will suffice.)

Wherefore he is able also to save them to the uttermost that come unto God by Him, seeing he ever liveth to make intercession for them.

HEBREWS 7:25, KJV

Read Job 1. Record every question and identify who asked it.

We'd all agree that most of the chapter is disturbing, but what parts do you find particularly discomforting?

Now read the second chapter of Job. Record the question Job's wife asked him and the question he asked her in response.

Job's wife:

Job's response:

R. L. Alden explains, "In the prologue the readers are informed of something that Job never learned, that is, that he was a test case. We know that he was innocent. God knows that he was innocent. Satan knows that he was innocent. The friends who came to counsel him were sure he was not innocent. Job was quite certain of his innocence, but even sane people begin to question their sanity when faced with excruciating losses and prolonged illness."[7]

Now read the poetry of Job 3. Record lines you find most moving or compelling.

Record the tremendously significant summation about Job found at the end of Job 2:10 and 42:7.

Repeat those statements to yourself in today's lesson and tomorrow's. Job did not sin in what he said. And he said a lot. After Job's friend, Eliphaz, lectured him in chapters 4 and 5, Job replied in chapters 6 and 7.

Read Job 6:24-26. How would you translate his point?

The ESV translates verse 26, "Do you think that you can reprove words, when the speech of a despairing man is wind?" I had the privilege of hearing Dr. John Piper preach from this text. He gave his own unforgettable paraphrase of Job 6:26. "Don't lecture me on my language when I'm in pain!" Dr. Piper termed this language of the despairing "wind words."[8] They need an outlet, not a lecture. They need to be given to the wind by both hearer and speaker.

Read Job's heart-wrenching questions in 3:11-12. Have you ever asked something similar? If so, recall to God what brought you to those existential questions.

Write Christ's words in Luke 12:6-7, and let them find a fresh place in you today.

Every part of your life is precious to God, including your physical body. Your skin (every freckle and scar), your chromosomes, your eye color, the length of your fingers and toes, the way you squint and smile, the way you look when you sleep: all precious to God. You are not only an immaterial being. You are also clay on the wheel of the Potter. Your matter matters. Though your body is temporal, it is not trivial. Though it is "lowly" (Phil. 3:21, ESV), it is still holy.

Use this space to thank God for your physical body and ascribe value to it. Get creative and detailed in what you thank Him for—taste buds, for instance, or the way your pillow feels on your face when you crawl in bed at night.

Read Hebrews 10:5-10. This segment quotes Jesus in reference to His own earthly body, borrowing words He Himself planted on a psalmist's tongue centuries earlier (Ps. 40:6-8).

Write His words from Hebrews 10:5-7.

Now read Hebrews 10:11-18. Record the "I will" statements of Christ in verses 16-17.

As your concluding prayer, pen the words of Psalm 40:8,11,13.

4.4

The dramatic twist in the Book of Job occurs just about the time the reader has surrendered to the discomfiting pattern of Job's friends' pious speeches and his intermittent defenses. Thirty-seven chapters into the book, not only is the reader growing weary of hearing from Job's friends, one gets the feeling that God Himself has heard enough.

Read Job 38:1-3 and describe God's approach.

Who did the Lord answer according to Job 38:1?

When God "answered" Job in 38:1, who exactly had just been speaking? Peruse the preceding chapters, watching for names and chapter headings to find your answer.

How many chapters had his speech endured?

Read Job 32:1-18. Why had Elihu waited until now to speak?

What did Elihu presume to do in Job 36:1-2?

When was the last time you winced over voices in the public square claiming to speak on God's behalf?

Job had not spoken since his last claims of innocence in chapters 30–31, yet 38:1 tells us explicitly that God answered Job rather than Elihu who'd tried to set the suffering man straight for six solid chapters. Never mind that Elihu was still wet behind the ears. The theology prodigy had just enough insight to be dangerous. He was articulate enough to attract attention but not mature enough to avoid presumption. Of course, presumptuousness is no respecter of age because aging, unfortunately, does not guarantee maturing. All it usually guarantees is gray hair. Anyone, young or old, can drum up the right facts but still draw the wrong conclusions.

Imagine God, whose voice sprung planets into existence and spun them into orbit, sitting on His throne listening to human tongues wag endlessly on His behalf. The complicated part is that we who know Christ really are called to testify and to communicate His gospel, so a gag order is not the answer. Neither is keeping your mouth shut until you're forty.

We who know Christ really are called to testify and to communicate *His gospel.*

What do you think the balance is? Offer your thoughts.

I think back over some of the words that have tumbled from my mouth while on a platform and wonder why God didn't jerk out my tongue or at least stuff a pair of knee socks in my mouth. I feel like I spend eighty percent of my time at the podium talking and the other twenty percent apologizing for what I said. Some of my mistakes have been spontaneous, but others, I'm ashamed to say, were part of my prepared notes. Somehow what seems OK in lifeless ink on a cold white page prints out a whole different way on parchments made of warm faces and soft hearts.

Often the issue isn't about whether the words are fair, accurate, or true. Sometimes they are just out of place or outside their opportune time. Issuing an appropriate apology is not to win back approval. Nothing will snap our tongues into a more dangerous trap than manipulating our words to gain human approval.

Galatians 1:10 warns us that we cannot strive to please both God and man. Our knees will bow to one or the other. If we're called to communicate and share the truth of God's Word, we are bound to say unpopular or offensive things at times, but let it be because the Holy Spirit spoke through us and not that we spoke for Him. Ephesians 4:29 is a fog-clearer especially in the ESV: "Let no corrupting talk come out of your mouths, but only such as is good for building up, as fits the occasion, that it may give grace to those who hear."

To dispense grace in this grace-parched culture is to offer a canteen in a desert.

Note the wording "only such as is good for building up." Building up is not the equivalent of pleasing and making happy. Sometimes the things we want most to hear would rip our lives to shreds. Other times, it is precisely what first offends that, second, mends. Grace only tears down for the sake of building up. We've all had some relationships, practices, or false beliefs that had to be torn down in order for us to be built up in the Spirit. Sometimes our pride has to be torn down so that our character can be built up. Sometimes our neglected health has to get torn down before we get serious enough to build it back up.

What comes to your mind regarding things God has torn down in order to build you up?

What conclusions can be drawn from the wording "as fits the occasion"?

Loop back to Job 38:1-3 and write verse 3 in this space.

By now you'll have no trouble spotting why this portion made it into our quest. The titanic twist in the plot of Job is that God remains silent through a veritable debate tournament showcasing more questions concerning God than a seminary final. But suddenly, God whips into the scene through a whirlwind and nearly buries Job alive in question marks. I love this commentary excerpt by J. E. Hartley:

"Without discounting Job's moral integrity, Yahweh challenges Job's perception of his governance of the world. By opening with the words *Who is this?* Yahweh asserts his superiority. Moreover, he shows respect for Job by addressing him as a virile *man* (*geḇer*). This choice of words means that neither his affliction nor his inflamed rhetoric has diminished his intrinsic worth as a human being ... Accepting Job's challenge to settle their differences, Yahweh summons him to gird up his loins. Job is enjoined to prepare himself as though they were to have a wrestling match. 'Girding the loins' means literally tucking in the skirt of the robe in one's belt; this is done so that one can work unhindered. It symbolizes pulling together all one's strength in order to wrestle energetically with a difficult task. In this match God will address questions to Job and expect an answer."[9]

Glance back at the excerpt. What does Dr. Hartley suggest Job "is enjoined to prepare himself" for?

Sound familiar? If so, in what way?

The match in Genesis 32:24-30 engaged the two opponents physically. The one in Job engages the two theologically. Make no mistake, a theological wrestling match can get just as personal as a physical wrestling match, and in some ways be just as bruising.

When was the last time you were part of a theological wrestling match, and what was the issue?

Here's a forecast you can count on: if God is the opponent in that match, He's always going to win, and (read this carefully) we're always going to be glad. Not once will we lose a wrestling match to God that leaves us a loser. His win is our win every time because we are His children. God cannot be wrong, nor can He be right yet do us wrong.

We're incapable of setting the bar high enough to estimate God. The outer limits of all human language and intelligence offer no adequate measuring stick. He alone is completely accurate about Himself. God also overhears the claims ungodly people make about Him.

Of what does Jude 15 say He will convict the ungodly?

Interesting, isn't it? Spreading harsh press about God is no small offense to Him.

Return to Job, and read God's indomitable questionnaire to His servant in Job 38:4-41.

If you can keep from losing count, tally the number of questions here: ______
If you could sum up all those divine questions into one, what would the question be?

Now glide your index finger slowly down chapters 39–41 to glimpse a gushing stream of questions that seems to momentarily break the dam between heaven and earth, causing waves of divine data to crash over a slack-jawed human.

Read Job 42:1-6, and succinctly describe the man's reaction.

Read Job 42:7-17, and record the portion of the closing prose you find most remarkable.

I can hardly get past two words in Job 42:16. *Job lived.* We need go no further to stumble on a wonder. Job lived through the severest test of any human depicted in Scripture. Job lived through the accusations, assaults, and murderous ruinations from man's terrible, invisible foe. Job lived through the cataclysmic loss of all his children and the loss of his wife's faith. Job lived through oozing boils from the soles of his feet to the top of his head. Job lived through his friends' pious sermons, judgments, and presumptions. And Job lived through God Almighty answering him out of the tempest and switching places at the interrogation table to question him.

On a quest where we're willing to brave asking hard questions, we may also undergo times when God puts us in our place with such gale force, He nearly turns us into dust. Based on the story of Job, a fresh comeuppance doesn't necessarily indicate we were wrong to ask those questions. Sometimes it's an all-purpose reminder of who's God and who's not. It also guards us against pride when He's revealed Himself powerfully to us. This we can know in our bold inquisitions: we cannot help but underestimate God. We underestimate His wisdom, foreknowledge, power, patience, faithfulness, timing, holiness, sovereignty, affection, redemption, and intrinsic, immutable goodness. However highly we view Him, the Most High is higher.

However highly we view Him, the *Most High* is higher.

So the LORD blessed the last part of Job's life more than the first.

JOB 42:12

Job lived to see the day that life, joy, wellness, and laughter filled his home again and herds filled his pastures. Job lived 140 more years without ever having his question answered. Did he still wonder why he'd suffered so? If he was anything like us, probably. But, you see, all his whys didn't have to be erased for him to make it. All they needed was to be eclipsed.

Record any questions to God still alive and stirring in your mind regarding the Book of Job after reading its conclusion.

Read Job 29:1-6, and reflect on how easy it is to come to similar deductions regarding God's nearness. Contrast Peter's perspective in 1 Peter 1:7 and 4:12-16. Journal your deliberations to God.

Let the words of Jesus in these two verses bring comfort to you as you pen them.

John 14:1

John 14:27

Record what James 5:11 says about God in the context of Job's story.

Shift your thoughts momentarily from identifying with the role of sufferer in Job to identifying with the role of friend to the sufferer. Bring to Jesus the names of three people you know well who are presently enduring great difficulty. Briefly describe the causes of their pain and make specific petition for them.

If you find any of the three particularly difficult to comfort or support, share it with God, and try to articulate to Him what you believe increases the difficulty.

Talk to Jesus about the kind of comforter you want to be. Ask Him for what you need.

Shift back to the role of sufferer. Pray for someone who let you down at a time you desperately needed support and comfort. Ask God to richly bless him or her. If words were spoken that you've had a hard time forgetting or getting over, place them on the altar before God, know they have been heard by Him, and release them. If you haven't forgiven the person who said them, ask Jesus, by the power of His cross, to enable you to do so now.

Conclude by writing Job 19:23-27 and then reading it aloud to God.

4.5

How far would you travel to find what you seek? How many calluses would you be willing to wear on your feet? Jesus lit the sandals of His first followers with a charge that has become fuel to our own feet through this six-week quest.

Write Matthew 7:7.

Concepts we really want to stick with us require some repetition. Remember, no one in the New Testament took to the hot pursuit more patently than the apostle Paul.

> Not that I have already reached the goal or am already perfect, but I make every effort to take hold of it because I also have been taken hold of by Christ Jesus. Brothers and sisters, I do not consider myself to have taken hold of it. But one thing I do: Forgetting what is behind and reaching forward to what is ahead, I pursue as my goal the prize promised by God's heavenly call in Christ Jesus.
>
> **PHILIPPIANS 3:12-14**

He'd gotten a blinding glimpse of something he craved in full so that every drop of his remaining energy went into that solitary pursuit. *This one thing I do.* In God's ingenious creativity, He fashioned human passion for even more than winning the prize. He fashioned it for chasing the prize. We are clay vessels with internal combustion that long to be driven. When we are lit with holy fire, this Jesus whom we've already found becomes the glorious aim of unquenchable finding.

Tucked in the folds of ancient kings and chronicles we find a gutsy woman who set her compass due-north fourteen hundred arduous miles through an unforgiving desert to find what she sought. She will be our inspiration today.

Please read 1 Kings 10:1-13. Who was she? Why had she braved such an extensive trip?

The homeland of the queen was "ancient Saba (roughly modern Yemen)," an area in the Arabian Peninsula recognized by historians for its extravagant wealth.[11] Perhaps you'll be as fascinated as I to learn that "female rulers played important roles in pre-Islamic Arabia."[12] Women of their era knew nothing of the misogyny that would one day plague their progeny.

Search 1 Kings 10:1-13 again and record all evidence of the queen's interest exceeding man's wisdom and reaching toward God's.

Both the NIV and ESV report that the queen of Sheba came to test Solomon "with hard questions." The CSB reads, "The queen of Sheba heard about Solomon's fame connected with the name of the LORD and came to test him with riddles" (v. 1).

"'Hard questions' *(ḥîḏôṯ)* is generally translated 'riddles,' which were enigmatic sayings or questions that cloaked a deeper philosophical, practical, or theological truth. Arabic literature abounds in riddles and proverbs. They were a favorite sport and a way to test one's mettle. It would appear from the following verses that the 'riddles' or 'hard questions' posed by the queen were not mere frivolous tests of mental quickness but a genuine seeking for truths hidden in some of the enigmatic sayings known to her."[13]

The queen's questions had sparked her royal quest to Jerusalem and likely multiplied over the course of the long journey. Chances are, the questions also grew increasingly transparent, perhaps even existential. Long days in deserts have a way of doing that to a sojourner. We're told in 1 Kings 10:2 she "spoke to him about everything that was on her mind." I'd have a lot on my mind if I survived fourteen hundred miles of desert. Her questions found a fitting audience.

How did Solomon perform (1 Kings 10:3)?

Consider 1 Kings 10:4 carefully. After hearing all his answers, "the queen of Sheba observed all of Solomon's wisdom." What kinds of things did she observe?

Have you ever met anyone with impressive intellect but didn't seem to have a clue what to do with it? Wisdom, in part, is the ability to connect the dots between the intellectual and the practical. It's not just knowledge. Wisdom is knowing what to do with what you know. Wisdom not only deduces. It produces. It sooner or later bears fruit in some observable way.

Read 1 Kings 3:5-15, and document how Solomon became so exceptional.

Flip to the next page or two in your Bible and meditate on 1 Kings 4:29-34 long enough to absorb and appreciate its implications. Keeping in mind that God Himself gave Solomon his wisdom and understanding, to what variety of topics did these divine gifts extend according to 1 Kings 4:32-34?

Every field is God's. There is utterly nothing about which He does not know everything.
All the "ics" and "ologies," like ...
Mathematics, economics, acoustics, ethics, aerodynamics, athletics, aesthetics.
Biology, sociology, anthropology, psychology,
philosophy, geology, technology, etymology.
Go no further than Genesis 2 for glimpses of divine ecology and zoology.
Astronomy? He didn't just speak the stars into the sky. He called them all by name.
Ornithology? He wove feathers to flesh and not a sparrow falls without His knowing.
Meteorology? Skies mirroring oceans. Clouds double-billed to bring rain and cloak glory.
He appointed lightning to strike and snowflakes to float from the same atmosphere.
All sciences originate with Him.
Social science, agricultural science, political science, computer science, health science.
Chemistry, physics, earth and space science.
Science is not God's objection. Godlessness is.
Oceanography: whales fashioned so He could watch them frolic.
Sexuality: for man and wife's exquisite pleasure and human procreation.
Archaeology: the same God who conceals, at His will, reveals.
Medicine originated with the Great Physician.
Nutrition from the holy Dietician.
And music? Ah, music. Imagine life without it.
Notes took wings and flew to their score at the command of the divine Composer.
Symphonies found their soul-clutching sounds at the command of the divine Conductor.
The arts were inspired by the Artist Himself.
Colors, textures, dimensions, shades.
Writers found ink under the inspiration of the One called *Logos*, the Word.
Every great tale winks in this way or that at God's brilliant metanarrative.

For everything was created by Him, in heaven and on earth,
the visible and the invisible,
whether thrones or dominions or rulers or authorities—
all things have been created through Him and for Him.
He is before all things and by Him all things hold together.

COLOSSIANS 1:16-17

Solomon wrote in Proverbs 1:7, "The fear of the LORD is the beginning of ________________________" and, in Proverbs 9:10, "The fear of the LORD is the beginning of ______________________."

To revere God as author and giver of all knowledge and wisdom, to reject hubris, and to see oneself as a steward of divine impartation, protects the mortal heart from the mortal wound of insolent lostness. It is not just God's protection of His own glory, though it is that. It is God's protection of man, lest a mortal think himself a god only to realize to his peril or another's that he is not. Playing god has been, since the beginning of time, too great a burden for humans to bear. History has painfully and perilously chronicled what a poor god man makes.

But exceptional wisdom and knowledge should be appreciated. They are not to be ignored out of respect for God as if they are His competitors. He has no competitors. Wholly unthreatened, He owns what man pretends to claim. Surely someone asked the queen of Sheba upon her return if what she gleaned was worth twenty-eight hundred miles of howling desert, and surely, with a glimmer in her eye, she nodded. She'd come back the richer.

Such God-given brilliance surrounds us. Our lives have been changed for good by inventions, theorems, explorations, and discoveries. Our souls have found comfort and joy in artistry, design, music, and literature.

What comes to your mind as I mention these contributions to our lives and souls? What inspires you? What demonstrations of human brilliance have affected you?

Exult in these gifts of God. Marvel over them. "When the queen of Sheba observed all of Solomon's wisdom … it took her breath away" (1 Kings 10:4-5). Credit the Lord just as she did: "Blessed be the LORD your God!" (1 Kings 10:9). Credit Him whether or not the human instruments of brilliance ever do. Never forget the wellspring of all wisdom and knowledge.

Never forget the *wellspring* of all wisdom and knowledge.

Set the compass lastly to 1 Kings 11:1-10. What happened in Solomon's older age?

It is never too late for the wise to become fools. But as long as it is still today, it is never too late for the foolish to become wise.

Record the question in James 3:13.

Let Christ speak to you through the words that follow in James 3:13-18. Take notes from these verses here.

Read James 1:5-8, and let these verses lead you into prayer and petition especially for faith to believe you will receive.

Seeing giftedness in others is usually easier than seeing it in the mirror. Thank God for that because it tempers the ego. But today be bold enough to talk to your grace-Giver about areas of giftedness, talent, wisdom, skill, and knowledge He's entrusted to you. Acknowledge them to Him with thanksgiving. Ask Him to sanctify those gifts and invade them for His great glory. Then have the courage to ask Him to significantly grow and develop them.

What line of work are you in, or, if you are a student, what field of education? Remember, God is not only an expert in your field; He created the field. Do you need to be smarter than you are at your job or in your field of responsibility or education? ASK.

When you get glimpses of answered prayer and you realize God has taught you more than you could learn in a textbook and enabled you beyond your natural capacities, profusely thank Him, and ask Him to make you a faithful steward of divine gifting. If it happens soon, record your gratitude here.

Ask God to free you from bondage to specific meaningless distractions so that your growth in giftedness is unhindered by them.

Intercede for several exceptional people who do not know Jesus, nor do they credit God, the wellspring of all wisdom and knowledge.

Conclude today's query by allowing God to speak through Jeremiah 33:3. Write the verse here, and take Him up on it for a lifetime.

Take a moment and reflect on your quest so far. Look back over each day of study and journal a brief note about what spoke to you, what you learned, and what course corrections you need to make. Then, spend a moment in prayer, writing from your heart to the Lord as you move forward on this quest.

DAY 1

Truths I encountered:

What I learned about myself and Jesus:

Course corrections I need to make:

DAY 2

Truths I encountered:

What I learned about myself and Jesus:

Course corrections I need to make:

DAY 3

Truths I encountered:

What I learned about myself and Jesus:

Course corrections I need to make:

DAY 4

Truths I encountered:

What I learned about myself and Jesus:

Course corrections I need to make:

DAY 5

Truths I encountered:

What I learned about myself and Jesus:

Course corrections I need to make:

Lord, as I move forward ...

Five

Video and audio sessions available for purchase at LifeWay.com/TheQuest.

#QuestStudy

5.1

My first grandchild named me Bibby soon after he learned to talk. It was his way of pronouncing "BeeBee" and, as is often the birthright of firstborn grandchildren, his rendition stuck. He's a bright, blue-eyed, half-grown middle schooler these days. But if you asked him to name his favorite frequent memory-maker with his maternal grandmother, I'm pretty sure what he'd say: Bibby's Secret Closet. I started the game when he was five and his little sister was two and his littlest sister had not remotely entered the mind of their parents. Keith and I had moved into a new house that had a double-door closet in the hall with shelves that seemed to me the perfect place to hide surprises. I stocked it with all sorts of fun and inexpensive things ranging from specialty candies to puzzles, from games to race cars, from dolls and art supplies to toy projectiles, the latter of which are essential if your aim is to steal a little boy's heart.

The rules of the game were established from the start: under no circumstances could they ever peek inside that closet. Indeed, they could not so much as touch the doorknobs or the Secret Closet would turn into just any old closet with no secrets at all. They perished that thought as the worst possible fate, just as I hoped. We get to do generous amounts of life together, so we couldn't play our game each visit or surprise would turn into routine and spoil the joy and, per their wise parents, also spoil the children. Every three or four visits, I'd raise my eyebrows just so and say, "Anybody want to do Bibby's Secret Closet?" They'd pop up like jack-in-the-boxes and run to a certain spot at the end of the hall, and the game would be on.

I'd draw it out as long as possible, opening the doors and closing them quickly as if something had startled me. Then I'd peek back in the closet and around the door again, making faces and performing ridiculously silly antics. They'd shake with excitement from head to toe and squeal like Santa Claus was sliding down the chimney. All this for a treat or toy that often came from a dollar store. We have played our game countless times through the years, and, though Jackson and Annabeth are getting older and playing it cooler, their two-year-old sister being old enough to join in has given it fresh wind.

I made space for this story to serve up some food for thought:

Would it be the same joyful experience for the children if I called them on their way over, told them what prize or candy they were about to get, and handed it over the second they walked through the door? Why or why not?

Read Colossians 1:15–2:3. Write Colossians 2:2-3 in this space.

Underline Colossians 2:3 in your copy above.

Early in our quest I suggested that instant intimacy is not God's signature style for relationships. Study the Scriptures through and through and there's no mistaking the Lord's affinity for surprise disclosure. For the easiest evidence to spot, however, all you need is a glance at Scripture's start and finish. The Bible opens with God creating the universe out of nothingness over an ordered course of six days in Genesis and ends sixty-five entire books later with Revelation. In Greek, the word for *revelation* is ***apokálupsis*** meaning:

"Revelation, uncovering, unveiling, disclosure. One of three words referring to the Second Coming of Christ (1 Cor. 1:7; 2 Thess. 1:7; 1 Pet. 1:7,13). The other two words are ***epipháneia***, appearing (1 Tim. 6:14), and ***parousía***, coming, presence (2 Thess. 2:1). ***Apokálupsis***, a grander and more comprehensive word, includes not merely the thing shown and seen but the interpretation, the unveiling of the same. The ***epipháneiai***, appearances, are contained in the ***apokálupsis***, revelation, being separate points or moments therein. Christ's first coming was an ***epipháneia*** (2 Tim. 1:10); the second, an ***apokálupsis***, will be far more glorious."[1]

Lock your eyes on that final word, *glorious*, because it is the glimmering handprint that sets divine revelation eons apart from my opening parable. Bibby's Secret Closet is about unveiling a toy. ***Apokálupsis*** is about unveiling glory.

Read 2 Corinthians 3:7-18. Record every piece of good news this segment offers a Jesus follower regarding glory.

On this side of Christ's complete unveiling, where "for now we see through a glass, darkly" (1 Cor. 13:12, KJV), we lack the perfection to always enjoy God's way of hiddenness. These dark stretches on our journey may be unwelcome, but they offer wide-open, sweat-faced space for faith. It's the shadowy miles that take the temperature of our trust. For us to persevere or dare to grow in our love for God while we momentarily do not love His observable way is no small wound on the devil's brow. But we would be woefully remiss to only regard the hard side of mystery. It also has an incomparably beautiful side and you haven't hung around this long because you don't know it. The mystery is part of what we love. It is part of what we crave. It is part of what has kept some of us studying the same text and seeking the same God for decades. The very fact that we can't figure it all out is one reason we're still here. We long for exactly what we've got: a Lion we can't tame but we can trust.

The human mind equates the cessation of mystery as an indication of mastery. No one masters God. Glance at Proverbs 25:2 and record what it says.

As we await what will only be revealed in the light of Christ's face, what is at our fingertips in God's Word and what is discoverable of Him beyond are still more than we could exhaust in a lifetime. We can tremble in fear over all we can't see or revel in every speck we can, for "in Him are hidden all the treasures of wisdom and knowledge" (Col. 2:3).

Hidden. Not displayed. This is holy hide and seek. We dig and discover. It beats archaeology by a landslide because the words are still alive. Imagine digging up the fossil of a fish that can still swim. If we sit with empty arms crossed, pouting over what Jesus is apparently unwilling to show us, we forfeit laps spilling over with treasures He was happy to uncover. Buried treasures are planted right there in the soil of your path where you can seek them and find them. Treasures set for discovery on a holy timer to be a word in due season. Nothing on earth is like divine revelation. Nothing compares to the Holy Spirit quickening His own words, making them clean air to our pollution-congested lungs and making them lamplight to our clouded understanding. When we don't find what we seek, we still don't shut His Word empty-handed. Like rummaging through closets and drawers in our homes, we stumble on one meaningful thing looking for another.

Nothing on earth is like *divine* revelation.

Scripture is too high to get to the top of it. Scripture is too deep to get to the bottom of it. However, if we brave our brief lives walking, crawling, swimming, sitting, and wading right in the middle of it, we will gain more wisdom than the world's sages.

Keep pleading above all else for Jesus to show you glimpses of His glory, His kingdom, and His ways on the page, and, there in the periphery, He will always show you what you need to know about yourself. Make the most of seeking Jesus, and He will leverage every ounce you bring to the mix and will make the most of your life offering. You steward His gifts, and He will steward you. The breathtaking you the world needs to see is the one drenched to the bone in Jesus. You have no idea how gorgeous you are, soaked in the radiance of His glory. You don't have to go find yourself. Spend your life hunting Jesus down, and He'll make sure your full calling—start to finish—hunts you down. Seek Him with your whole being even if you're in a thousand pieces, and He will sweep you up in His unseen arms, equip you, grow you, develop you, and show you where to set your foot next.

For with you is the fountain of life; in your light we see light.

PSALM 36:9, NIV

Your dialogue today will center on divine treasures "for where your treasure is, there your heart will be also" (Matt. 6:21). By this point in your six-week quest, you've gotten the rhythm of query. So this week you'll get to set your own metronome a good bit before you head off by yourself. All the Scriptures below revolve around treasures. Read each one and let it become a catalyst for prayer. The verses are so rich, you shouldn't have a difficult time. If God uses the verse to inquire of you, write down what you believe to be the question and answer it. If, on the other hand, the verse stirs up petitions you desire to ask of God, write them down and expound on them. If one makes you recall something He's done for you, tell Him about it. If one voices exactly how you feel, tell Jesus that.

Psalm 119:162

Proverbs 24:3-6

Pray no less passionately if you live alone than you would if your walls were bulging with a large family. You are building a "house" wherever you call home.

Isaiah 33:6

Isaiah 45:3

Matthew 13:44

Matthew 13:52

In Matthew 13:52, Jesus likens a disciple of the kingdom of heaven to a household master who gathers an assortment of new and old treasures from a storage room. This disciple has in view the full landscape of heaven's kingdom, not naively discarding the old things out of sheer enthusiasm for the new but allowing the new to reframe the old in unexpected ways. As R. T. France puts it,

"The message of the kingdom of heaven does not wipe the slate clean, but rather brings fulfillment to what has gone before, as Jesus has been at pains to demonstrate in [Matthew] 5:17-48. The 'old' is not to be 'abolished' (5:17), but to be judiciously integrated into the new perspective of the kingdom of heaven."[2]

Every time you pick up a Bible—complete with its two testaments—you hold in your hand treasures new and old. The life of faith is a mysterious combination of both. In Christ, a new treasure never devalues an old one. All get to be yours. Sometimes what you considered treasure early in your walk with Him seems childish and unsophisticated later, but it needn't. Those things were dear to you. Cherish them. Reflect back on some old treasures and recount at least one to God.

Write out the exquisite words of Psalm 36:5-9 in any translation you like as your concluding prayer.

5.2

Equipping ourselves to embrace life as a quest calls for the brave, biblical acknowledgment that the road is hazardous, the weather precarious, obstacles await, and evils lurk. Perilous traveling conditions are not automatic indications we've taken a detour. Sometimes they are highway signs saying we're on the right track. A glamorous gospel is not just deceptive. It is tragic. It turns grace into sensuality, and then offers no remedy for sin's bankruptcy. A glam-gospel is the crowd-pleaser of the short run, but in the long run when sufferings inevitably come, it abandons us as orphaned children, leaving us believing God broke His promises.

Following Jesus is the *ultimate* long run.

Following Jesus is the ultimate long run. The muscle it demands is built with protein-packed doctrine believable and sustainable from beginning to end—in celebration and sorrow, exhilaration and malaise, in days of crisp, clear vision, and in nights so black you can't see your feet. To unplugged ears, the New Testament testifies with deafening volume to the role of adversity and the demand for endurance in the lives of disciples on their sure way to happily ever after. Sometimes God Himself sets up an obstacle course to develop and test the runner's discipline, stamina, and agility. With His eye around every blind curve in our road ahead, He seeks "to supply what is lacking in [our] faith" (1 Thess. 3:10, ESV) so we can run triumphantly.

Satan also attends to our marathon with unanticipated patience, biding his time, studying our patterns and weaknesses. He tempts runners nearby to go rogue and trip us. He'll incite spectators to mock us. He'll harass us with regrets and torment us with self-condemnation until we feel like quitting. He'll cover us in shame till we feel like we're running naked. He'll try to sell us anger and hate relabeled as holy passion. He'll camouflage potholes with pretties to coax us into pits. If we manage to dodge them, he'll try to wear us down gradually with discouragement. If we don't wear down easy, he'll tempt us to perform valiantly and with impressive false humility for the applause of an audience we pretend to ignore. And we will fall for some of it. But that's the beauty of running a path paved by a cross and sprinkled with blood. We can get back up.

Do not rejoice over me, my enemy! Though I have fallen, I will stand up. Though I sit in darkness, the LORD will be my light.

MICAH 7:8

So, here's the point of today's Compass: on a journey fraught with spills, we can access incomparable thrills. Since we can't avoid difficulties and sufferings, we can ask, seek, and knock with everything in us for every gorgeous thing that is ours in Christ, so that we not only can bear up in this race, we can shockingly thrive in it. No, we will not always have fun, but, based on the authority of God's Word, we can always abound.

And God is able to make all grace abound to you, so that having all sufficiency in all things at all times, you may abound in every good work.

2 CORINTHIANS 9:8, ESV

Underline the words *all* and *every*. Circle the word *abound*. Want to see its Greek definition?

perisseúō; from ***perissós***, abundant. To be in excess, exceed in number or measure. In the NT, to be or have more than enough. (I) To be left over, remain, exceeding a number or measure which marks fullness … (II) To superabound, to abound richly.[3]

Glance back at the additional Greek word in the definition—*perissós*. What one English word is offered to define it?

You'll find a form of this word translated in John 10:10. Read John 10:7-10 for context. In His own words, why had Jesus come?

What we're having today is not a pep talk. It's not a lesson chock-full of feel-good aphorisms that have the shelf life of an overripe peach swarming with fruit flies. We have birthrights in Christ that can inject curious happiness into copious hardships. Let's fight for them. Let's fight for the things that make following Jesus so gloriously good that the sufferings won't even be worth comparing (Rom. 8:18). Let's fight for …

AUDACIOUS LOVE

ECSTATIC JOY

UNABASHED DELIGHT

ASTONISHING FAITH

UNQUENCHABLE HOPE

EXTRAORDINARY FRUITFULNESS

OVERFLOWING GRATEFULNESS

The list is not exhaustive by any means, but these seven are enough to revolutionize our journey. Remember back in Week Four, Day One when I told you that we'd get to the subject of healthy consolations before our quest was over? Today's the day.

All seven of those divine graces—love, joy, delight, faith, hope, fruitfulness, and gratefulness—are generously supported in the Bible as the will of God for His children. Our lesson will only make room for a few under each category so chase others down with a Bible concordance for proof. The choice of adjectives—audacious, ecstatic, unabashed, astonishing, unquenchable, extraordinary, and overflowing—are showcased in multiple scenes in Scripture. Anyway, "superabounding" seems to make elbowroom for certain superlatives as does our fifth recalibrating question, *how much more?* It's no harder for God to give us a pound of something He wants us to possess than to give us an ounce. James 4:2 says, "you do not have because you do not ask." We've got mounds of problems. We may as well take God up on heaps of privileges.

Look up the verses in each category and document how they support the heading. If the number of verses seems overwhelming, it will help to know they also cover today's Query.

AUDACIOUS LOVE

God's supreme desire for us is that we love Him supremely (Mark 12:28-30). Love drives every vertical virtue in the believing life. If Jesus is the uncontested love of your life, you will follow Him, enjoy Him, obey Him, believe Him, find comfort and refreshment in Him, and long to see Him. Love also informs the lateral virtues of the believing life like compassion, forgiveness, generosity, and kindness. "Love does no wrong to a neighbor" (Rom. 13:10). Love makes sharing Christ with others virtually irresistible. It's hard to stay silent about the transcendent love of your life. Love shifts our motivations toward Jesus from what we need to do to what we want to do. To be sure, need is a vital motivator, but nothing compels the human heart like fervent desire. We would run barefoot through a briar patch for love.

The capacity to love God comes from God. It boomerangs right back to Him from the heart that fully catches it. We love Him because He first loved us (1 John 4:19). Your security and stability in Him and much of your fidelity toward Him are vastly dependent on whether or not you embrace as fact that you are personally, completely, and unequivocally loved by God. God is love. He could no more cease to love than He could cease to be God.

Before you search the verses regarding your love for Him, meditate on the profoundness of John 15:9. To what did Christ compare His love for His followers?

Now proceed to verses regarding audacious love for God.

Ephesians 6:24

1 Peter 1:8a

ECSTATIC JOY

Psalm 4:7

Psalm 16:11

Psalm 43:4

1 Peter 1:8b

UNABASHED DELIGHT

An obvious question regarding this heading is why we wouldn't throw delight into the joy category. They're similar enough. The simple answer is because God references both as if they are somehow distinct yet each greatly desirable. If your translation for each of the following verses doesn't contain the word *delight*, try another. It's too wonderful a word to miss.

Psalm 37:4 (Note the mutual delight in 37:23-24.)

Jeremiah 15:16

Bask in Psalm 18:19, "He brought me out to a spacious place;
He rescued me because He delighted in me."

ASTONISHING FAITH

Matthew 15:28

Hebrews 11:32-35

Write the four fabulous staccato exhortations of 1 Corinthians 16:13 here.

UNQUENCHABLE HOPE

Romans 5:5

Romans 15:13

Hebrews 6:10-12,19

EXTRAORDINARY FRUITFULNESS

John 15:8

Colossians 1:10

OVERFLOWING GRATEFULNESS

Colossians 2:6-7 (CSB, NIV, and NASB use the actual adjective "overflowing.")

Grateful people are the loveliest humans on planet Earth. They smile easy, eyes crinkling, like they know something the rest of us don't. They delight easy. They manage to retain a certain playfulness and childlike sense of wonder that make them sparkle like fireflies in a world of hornets.

As we traverse an earth that is groaning for redemption, we're going to run into toils, troubles, persecutions, tears, losses, heartaches, and grief. These difficulties may dash us, but they cannot defeat us if we fight for audacious love, ecstatic joy, unabashed delight, astonishing faith, unquenchable hope, extraordinary fruitfulness, and overflowing gratefulness. These surpluses of grace in this perilous race whisper what it means for weak mortals to show themselves "more than conquerors" (Rom. 8:37).

I don't have the luxury of writing these things from a loft in Cinderella's castle. I would like to have lived a sheltered life, but I haven't. Some of the reasons I share publicly. Some I don't. Some of my challenges are ongoing consequences of sins and foolish decisions made long ago. Others are sacred trusts drawing me deeper into intimacy with God. I can't say I always know which is which. Six solid decades I've plodded and plowed my life path, and little of it has come easy, yet I'll tell you something from the truest place in my heart. Had Jesus, at any point in the last thirty years, given me a thirty-second heads-up that He was about to sweep me home, I'd have used it to say one thing:

I have had the biggest blast with You.

Stumbling around on our stony paths and falling facedown in the soil, sometimes we accidentally uncover a secret to contentment we didn't even know to search for: God's highest Treasure is our greatest pleasure. Augustine gives voice to that truth:

> "How sweet all at once it was for me to be rid of those fruitless joys which I had once feared to lose ... ! You drove them from me, you who are the true, the sovereign joy. You drove them from me and took their place, you who are sweeter than all pleasure ... you who outshine all light, yet are hidden deeper than any secret in our hearts, you who surpass all honour, though not in the eyes of men who see all honour in themselves ... O Lord my God, my Light, my Wealth, and my Salvation."[4]

As you near the end of this quest, you will hear echoes of the five recalibrating questions that launched this stretch of your journey. Perhaps they will stir up the same answers you recorded over four weeks ago. If so, own them honestly before God, knowing your quest with Him extends well beyond this series. If they differ in any way, take note of the differences and reflect on them with God. They will be significant for your road ahead.

Revisit the third recalibrating question. You'll find it in John 1:38. Record Christ's question here:

Glance back over those seven graces in today's Compass. Thumb through earlier pages of this study. Four weeks have come and gone since this precise question was posed to you.

Tell Jesus in the space below what you're seeking now. If you know based on the Word that what you're asking is God's will, be bold enough to thank Him in advance. It's coming.

5.3

Your life is the stuff of great adventure. It may not feel that way when you're taking out the trash or treating the dog for fleas, but it really is. In all the mess and in all the mundane, you are a living, breathing miracle. You once were dead, but you were raised to new life. You were poor, but someone's death left you rich. Now your inheritance awaits you in a furnished home you've never seen in a land on no man's map. You once were blind, but now you can see. You were deaf to hope, but now you can hear.

You're headed home, but you have no idea how long the trip will take. You've been assigned tasks on your way that you don't fully understand, plus they demand strength your bones do not possess. Instead of being clothed in an invisible choir robe and halo, you were handed a soldier's uniform and shown in the Scriptures that your path unfolds right down the middle of a battlefield with the darkness as your adversary. You don't feel particularly brave or important, yet you've been involved in matters of life and death. You have vile enemies belched from hell that you cannot see who are assigned to stop what you've been sent to do, and you have but one sword and one shield with which to defend yourself. All the while, you're going about life at a job, in a town, and maybe even in a home where most people don't realize who you are and handing small deposits to a bank teller who has no clue what you're worth.

If that's not the stuff of great adventure, nothing on God's green earth qualifies. This epic drama is not your imagination. Your imagination is running rife if you think this is all there is, that what you can see with your eyes is the greater reality, and that time is running out rather than running forward to the ultimate big event. Your imagination is running away with you if you think all you have to bring to the present battle is whatever you brought to the last and that fierceness in spiritual war can't be for the person with ghastly morning breath who stares back at you blankly from your bathroom mirror.

The needle of your compass will point one final time in our six-week quest to the apostle Paul. He is the New Testament poster child for life-on-quest and also fleshes out on the page the kinds of things that are possible for those who valiantly love, believe, follow, obey, and draw divine strength from the Lord Jesus Christ. His second letter to the church of Corinth is solid gold if we're searching for material that reads like journal entries from his great adventures.

Read the opening entry in 2 Corinthians 1:1-11. Describe the intensity of their hardships in Asia.

What two things had overflowed to them according to 2 Corinthians 1:5?

According to 2 Corinthians 1:8-9, what had the severity of their suffering caused Paul and his companions?

Some truths can't be absorbed theoretically. We don't know what God can do until no one else can do it. No chronicle of Paul's adventures is complete without 2 Corinthians 11:24-33. Imagine you are interviewing him for a podcast. What three accounts in his brief autobiography would you ask him to elaborate on?

1.

2.

3.

A friend of mine decided recently to get away from it all and go camping and hiking by herself. One night she lay shaking with fear while a bear sniffed around her tent for forty-five minutes. That kind of thing has a way of improving your prayer life. You may not have been beaten with rods, but you've probably faced dangers in the city and perhaps in the wilderness. You've been betrayed and endured toil and spent sleepless nights.

If you were writing an autobiography at this point in your life, what three events would you include? List them in the left column. In the right column beside those three events, record how God was involved in that part of your narrative from your perspective.

EVENTS	GOD'S INVOLVEMENT

You have a story underway and it is made up of three parts:

A. Christ's story;

B. Your story without Him;

C. Your story together.

If you haven't already done so, ask God to help you weave these story parts together and tell it. People need to hear it.

Every powerful "Part C: Your story together" will reflect some form of Paul's account in 2 Corinthians 4:1-18. Read this portion.

In 2 Corinthians 4:7, what did Paul say we have?

According to the same verse, why do we have it?

Let the wonder wash over you: we are basic, run-of-the-mill, breakable, crumble-prone jars of clay filled with the incomparable, inexhaustible, exquisite treasure of Jesus Christ. God purposed this holy juxtaposition of treasure and clay so that "this extraordinary power may be from God and not from us." Our unimpressiveness accentuates God's inestimable impressiveness. Let this sink in deeply: By God's unfathomable design your ordinary, everyday breakable self is a storage unit for extraordinary power.

How much difference does it make? Reread 2 Corinthians 4:7-9 and fill in the chart.

We may be …	But we are not …
v. 8a	
v. 8b	
v. 9a	
v. 9b	

According to 2 Corinthians 4:10,
We always carry …
so that …

Write 2 Corinthians 4:12 in this space.

OK. We've bumped up against one of the most mature aspects in the doctrine of suffering. We're a long way from pureed bananas on the baby food aisle on this one. We're in the meat department now, gnawing one of the hardest bones in the New Testament. The fact is, sometimes God may, with gracious forethought and faithful deliberation, allow us to go through something that nearly kills us so someone else can come alive. He alone is life giver, but He can use death at work in one person to demonstrate life at work to another. The Book of Acts, followed by centuries of Christian history, forbids us to ignore the cost at its highest price: following Christ has more than nearly killed many believers. These are martyrs called to the highest imitation of Christ.

He can use *death* at work in one person to demonstrate *life* at work to another.

What did He say about them in Revelation 2:10?

Jesus esteems every costly sacrifice. Each will be surpassed by reward.

Before we're engulfed with dread over the prospect of death at work in us, consider the possibility that you may have already lived through a measure of it so that life could work in someone else. Extreme circumstances in parenting, in battling injustice, or in mission work, for example, can take a servant of God beyond normative sacrificial living and giving into costs requiring severe death to self, health, or well-being.

Those in leadership who walk in cruciform obedience to Christ will almost certainly embrace such a calling. Have you ever experienced anything like this? Expound.

To stop the lesson here would be such a tragedy. Study 2 Corinthians 4:10-12. What reason did Paul repeatedly give for death working in the life of a servant of God?

In Christ, there's simply no staying dead. Resurrection life is compulsory. Death—no matter the form—never gets to be our benediction. When we're called to the kind of dying Paul described in 2 Corinthians 4, God's purpose is always for the very life of Christ to be manifested in us. That's the best shot people have to catch a glimpse of Jesus when they're not remotely looking for Him. Death at work in us so that life works in another sounds like a dismal earthly sentence with heavenly rewards alone. However, I'd like to suggest that some of those rewards are reaped right here on this planet.

Read 1 Thessalonians 3:6-9. Write verse 8 here.

I love the NASB: "For now we really live, if you stand firm in the Lord." Admit it. There are people we'd walk straight into flames for. We'd go through that death process a dozen times just to glance over at them in a worship service and see them rapturously captivated with Jesus. We'd hang by our ankles for a month to hear people we've served testify about what Jesus has come to mean to them. A total stranger could tell us how Christ in us affected them and we'd walk away, tears streaming down our cheeks, and whisper to Jesus, "I'd go through it all again with You just for her/him."

How did Paul testify to this phenomenon in Philippians 2:17-18?

I've experienced another kind of peculiar joy and heard others speak of it, too. In the handful of times I've been called to endure seasons that have all but killed me, for a while I might have existed putting one foot in front of the other, zombie-like. But when I'd finally started coming back to life, I'd invariably feel more alive than before. Ordinary things I'd taken for granted in my busyness were suddenly like lush gifts. I'd close my eyes and savor a gentle breeze across my face. I'd stare in wonder at a pill bug forging a blade of grass that seemed a whole new shade of green. I wouldn't just see the colors of my children and grandchildren's eyes, I'd see the subtle flecks in their irises. A song wouldn't just move me, it would make me sob. Instead of dodging the rain, I'd close my umbrella, hold my head back and let it bathe my face, washing away invisible stains of the last hundred tears. Each time I've wished I could hang onto that vivid awareness of life forever, but soon it's back to life as usual. Then again, that's what eternity is for.

One day there will be no going back to life as usual. One day there will be no more night and no more dying of any kind. The sea and the grave, death and Hades will have given up their dead and the righteous Judge will have assigned final destinies (Rev. 20:11-15). When that eternal day comes I suspect we who were saved from our sins by the blood of Christ will ponder this life and wonder how we ever really called it "being alive."

Rewind to Genesis 3 and read the chapter until you come upon the first of this journey's five recalibrating questions. It is the first divine question in a list from the Bible that, by Revelation's closing, would tally to multiple hundreds. Write it here:

You answered this question in the first day's query. Now answer afresh where you sense you are spiritually, but this time use Paul's words in 2 Corinthians 4:8-9 as a paradigm.

Bringing where you see yourself spiritually into alignment with Scripture is crucial on the quest of faith. It increases stability and forward mobility. How you feel is important. The psalmists often and openly expressed their feelings about how bleak or triumphant their situations seemed. Framing your spiritual condition with the Word of God, however, changes how you see the picture.

Fill in the following lines from 2 Corinthians 4:8-9 to express concepts similar to Paul's, but use your own words and specifics to personalize it.

God,

I am ________________________________

but not ________________________________ .

I am ________________

but not ________________.

I am ________________

but not ________________.

I am ________________

but not ________________.

Write 2 Corinthians 4:13.

____

____

Second Corinthians 4:7-13 depicts the kind of dying that works in a believer to bring Christ's life to full breath in you. Think of 2 Corinthians 4:13 as divine CPR in the process of resurrection life when death has been at work in you. With "the same spirit of faith … we also believe, and therefore speak." The word translated *spirit* is *pneuma* in the Greek text, meaning *breath*.

pneuma **(*pneúma*; gen. *pneúmatos*, neut. noun from *pnéō*) … to breathe. (I) Breath. (A) Of the mouth or nostrils, a breathing, blast … (B) Breath of air, air in motion, a breeze, blast, the wind … (II) Spirit. (A) The vital spirit or life, the principle of life residing in man.[5]**

When you read the Scriptures, believing them with that same spirit of faith Paul talked about, think of the process as inhaling. Then when you speak them, think of the process as exhaling. Get the idea? Nothing supplies more divine oxygen on your quest than breathing in Scripture by faith. Subsequently, nothing applies power to your feet like breathing Scripture out through speech.

Practice the approach with 2 Corinthians 4:8-9. 1) Read it, believing and receiving it by faith, and then 2) speak it aloud with boldness. Countless segments await you in Scripture that can give you spiritual CPR when life is nearly killing you.

Have you experienced a time when God brought you back to life after a death of sorts had been at work in you? If so, recount it to God, including any way life seemed more vivid or precious to you.

Read 2 Corinthians 4:16-18 aloud in first person, switching "we" to "I." Testify to Jesus what glories are happening in your life amid these short-lived pains.

Lastly, look back over your answer in your very first query to the question "Where are you?" (p. 16) If you feel you've shifted or moved at all in the last five weeks, express it to God. If not, petition Him to move you where you want to be in Him.

Drag barely beating heart
dulled by woes and foes
and scarred
by worldly flames awry
to your God awaiting
and there by unseen hand
be raised.

5.4

The needle on the compass today points a direction deliberately timed for your next-to-last day. My hope is that, long after this six-week quest is complete, this site on the journey will be one you remember best. Taking the advice we will overhear Jesus give a dearly loved follower will become a crescendo to our contentment, drowning out untold contentiousness.

Read and relish John 21 like breakfast on the beach with the resurrected Jesus. Record each question in the chapter even if the same question is posed repeatedly.

How perfectly fitting for John's Gospel to conclude with questions volleying between Christ and His disciples. That's exactly the way it began. Remember these from John 1:35-51?

> What are you seeking?
>
> Where are you staying?
>
> Can anything good come out of Nazareth?
>
> How do you know me?
>
> Do you believe because I told you I saw you under the fig tree?

Life with Christ has more full-circle moments than a bowl of Cheerios®. In John 21 we get to witness the apostle Peter drenched in redemption in front of his peers. The only thing he's more famous for than walking on water with Jesus is denying

Him three times. Up until the denial, Peter had practically been the star of the class. A little showy maybe, but stars can sometimes be like that. By the time the camera hits him in John 21, we have a humbler version of Peter. We love the earlier version in Matthew 14, where he has the audacity to shout over the storm, "Lord, if it's you, command me to come to you on the water" (v. 28). But, if we're willing to appreciate a subtler wonder, the post-failure version of Peter is equally compelling. We get the feeling John barely got the words "It is the Lord!" out of his mouth before Peter plunged in the water and swam for dear life to Jesus. Further, instead of lightening his load for a sleeker swim, he grabbed his outer cloak and put it back on. More modesty, less showiness. More listening, less yakking. More Jesus-confidence, less me-confidence. In Christ's upside-down kingdom, those are upgrades.

Today's compass setting offers us an opportunity to underscore a previous point and establish a new one. Let's underscore first. Never one to waste words, by the time Jesus is asking the same question three times, He's tapping His spoon on a glass to get the attention at the table. Most theologians nod to the probability that the number of times Christ asked Peter if he loved Him was intended to match the number of times Peter denied Him. A do-over: same man, same mouth, same subject (Jesus), opposite outcome. If that is a new thought to you, don't move past it quickly. Savor the splendid redemption. The distinct way Jesus pairs affection and vocation in the scene also drums the point we've touched on in our quest: the single greatest motivator for our obedience to His calling is our tremendous affection for Him.

Simon, son of John, do you love me more than these?

Yes, Lord, you know that I love you.

Feed my lambs.

Then again. And again.

Tuck this somewhere easily accessible in your memory: the harder the obedience, the harder you pray for love. Don't just pray to be strong. Pray to love Jesus more than anyone or anything else on this earth, believing to your core that the best thing you could do for all others in the long run is to love Him most. The path of least resistance in a hard act of obedience is the one that has been forged ahead by love. When Jesus has so thoroughly captivated you that to follow Him is to follow your heart, the pure romance of your quest will take you places the bravest adventurer would fear to tread.

Now, onto the new point. You no doubt caught the million dollar question Peter asked Jesus in John 21:21: "Lord, what about him?" Few things on the quest of faith will trip us up more often than comparing ourselves with others in eyeshot. And social media has offered us an ocean-wide eyeshot. When our heads are whipping side to side, it's hard to focus on the way ahead. When we judge by appearances or compared experiences based on partial understanding at best, we will sooner or later come to the conclusion that Jesus isn't fair. The problem is, it's hard to measure grace by a fair yardstick.

Notice Peter asks the question once, but John quotes the answer twice:

Verse 22: "what is that to you?"

Verse 23: "what is that to you?"

Loose translation? "That, Peter, is none of your business."

And yet that trips us up over and over. "Jesus, why didn't you call me to that?" "Why didn't you give me a gift like that?" "Why didn't it work out for me like that?" "Why can't I have success like that or a ministry like that?" "Why can't I find love like that?" "Why didn't my marriage go like that?" "Why aren't my kids like that?" "Why couldn't I look like that?" "Why isn't my health like that?" "Why couldn't your plans for me have been like that?"

Want to add a few examples?

The answer is left dangling at the Gospel's end on the hook of a question mark: *What is that to you?* In this competitive culture we live in, that seems to be everything. The flip side of the question "what about him/her?" is "what about me?" That one coin flips continually in the grimy hand of comparison. If we don't want to be driven to distraction on our quest, tripping constantly, knees and elbows skinned and bloody, competition may require more than resistance. With sibling rivalry making a public laughingstock of the family of Christ, it needs renouncing. Fellow believers are meant to be companions, not competitors. They are intended to be dearly loved joys and crowns to us (Phil. 4:1) as our sandals flap through thorny soil. They are comforts on a globe aflame with fear and whirling with anxiety.

How do the following segments illustrate this truth?

2 Corinthians 7:5-7	Colossians 4:10-11

In a world where Jesus followers often feel alienated, we can run to one another, huddle, laugh, and muse for a moment and almost taste home.

Whose company gives you what you think might be a foretaste of heaven's fellowship? Name several people.

We squirm for the apostle Peter in John 21:21 because we'd have wondered *What about* ________________?, too, even if we dearly loved the other follower. Peter surely loved John dearly. Perhaps he simply wondered if he got the short straw over the denial. The irony is that John may have had questions of his own in regard to the others when he was banished to Patmos. He was the only one of the Twelve left on earth. The others had gotten to offer their lives in martyrdom and were safely in the presence of their dearest Love. In what surely was nearly unbearable isolation, under the beating sun with old, aching bones, don't you imagine the beloved disciple wondered, *Why didn't Your plan for me go like that? What on earth am I doing here?* Then one shocking Lord's day, he got a glimpse (Rev. 1:9-10). We may catch a glimpse this side of the veil why Christ's plan for us didn't mirror someone else's, but we will not truly understand until we're in His presence. Perhaps right there at the marriage supper of the Lamb, we will see the Bride of Christ in her fullness, put completely together, lacking nothing, and we will marvel over the brilliant lace of a billion threads, not one left hanging.

Return to John 21:22. Record Christ's directive to Peter and take it as personally as you would if you were eye to eye.

Here's what you have to give Jesus that no one else on earth can give Him: your faithfulness. You follow Him. Cheer others on with lavish generosity and all the more when there is no reciprocity. Encourage, assist, bless, and celebrate others. Esteem them above yourself without hating yourself. Jealousy and rivalry are relentless bloodhounds on the quest, smelling blood in every whiff of insecurity. Let's quit giving off the scent.

In John 13:1-17, Christ slack-jawed His disciples (none more so than Peter) by getting up from the supper table, tying a towel around His waist, pouring water into a basin, and washing their filthy feet.

Why did He do such a thing according to John 13:14-15?

What question did Jesus ask them in John 13:12?

The CSB words the question to perfection: "Do you know what I have done for you?" Reflect on the profoundness of Christ's question as one of His present followers. Consider your own answer in terms of the immediate context of John 13:1-17 and Christ's similar teachings.

Do you know what He has done for you by calling you ...

to serve rather than be served?

to humility rather than hubris?

to the feet of others rather than over their heads?

to the high road of loving your enemies and blessing those who curse you?

to dispense grace when the natural inclination would be to shame and blame?

to practice mercy over judgment?

Consider the manifold wisdom of Jesus and what a favor He's done His followers. Let the question marinate a moment then put pen to paper to answer it. Let it fall directly on you by writing your name in this blank:

Do you know what I have done for you, ____________________?

In all likelihood, there are people with whom you're either competition-prone or competition-thrown. The latter refers to comparisons others make between you and someone else. Spectators love competitions so they fuel the fight. Refuse to entertain them. Talk to Jesus and ask Him to help you identify the triggers, to deliver you from the temptation to enter the contest, and to empower you to persist in victory even if others keep competing. Ask Him to replace any envy you have for another person with genuine appreciation and affection.

Perhaps no one in the New Testament was put to a harder "what about me?" test than John the Baptist. He was the forerunner of Jesus and related by blood. John had baptized Jesus and sent his own disciples to follow Him, yet Jesus did not show up to rescue John from prison. He was performing magnificent signs and wonders elsewhere. Jesus said of John, "Truly I tell you, among those born of women no one greater than John the Baptist has appeared" (Matt. 11:11), but He did not stop John's beheading. Did Jesus even care? Matthew 14:13 reports that, "When Jesus heard about it, he withdrew from there by boat to a remote place to be alone." John knows now why he didn't get the miraculous intervention others did, and Romans 8:18 has become his living, breathing reality. Can you imagine the reunion between Jesus and John? It is unthinkable that he would have said in retrospect, "If I had it to do all over again, I'd still want to be somebody else." It is easier to imagine a man who'd made a wardrobe of camel's hair and a diet of locusts singing "O for a thousand heads to give."

Trust Jesus when everybody seems to be getting a miracle but you. When you feel forsaken and yet remain faithful, you are the miracle.

Write Christ's words in Matthew 6:6.

No matter what anyone has that you don't have, no one gets to have more of Jesus than you. No one gets to have more access to God than you. No one is more loved or cherished. No one gets to worship Him more, enjoy Him more, savor His words more, trust Him more, sing to Him more, or receive more of His warmth and comfort.

Turn for the final time in this six-week quest to Luke 11:13. Read it, then write the fifth recalibrating question. Then, Beloved of God, answer it.

5.5

We arrive today at a "Y" in the road after five weeks of walking out our quests within waving distance of one another with our compasses synced. That the grace of getting to serve has never lost its luster to me testifies both to the unforgettably muddy depths of defeat God pulled me out of and the immutable saving, cleansing, sanctifying power of Christ's cross. I don't know if I've worn you out or if God's Spirit invaded these pages as I prayed He would and made this quest energizing to you. On the very first day we discussed that, according to author J. L. Hancock's painstaking research, the KJV Bible is home to 3,298 questions.[6] The sum of questions in most formal translations would fall somewhere in the same ballpark. You may feel at this point that you've looked up all of them. You are a saint and I thank God for you.

To tie up our six-week quest without writing out your five recalibrating questions would be a travesty so, by all means, get to it.

"________________________________?" (Genesis 3:9)

"________________________________?" (Genesis 3:11)

"________________________________?" (John 1:38)

"________________________________?" (Matthew 8:26)

"________________________________?" (Luke 11:13)

I proposed that bringing candid, current answers to these five divine questions—not to diary, friend, pastor, teacher, or mentor but—straight to the One who originally asked them can potentially recalibrate and reignite a walk that has lost steam, gotten off track, or stuck in a cul-de-sac. I pray this will prove true. But, no matter what path you take, always know you can find intimacy with God again. Ask, seek, knock.

Early this week I told you that our final miles together would bump us back into all of the five recalibrating questions. We've already bumped into three: *What are you seeking? Where are you? How much more?* Before this lesson ends, you'll discover, *Who told you that?* In today's query, *Why are you afraid?* will reemerge. But let's talk a final time about the broader spectrum of questions beginning with the provocative, often bewildering word *why*. The path is too why-prone not to mention it again toward the end.

Why do you think our human minds are loaded with whys?

My husband, Keith, was famous in his family for his insatiable whys. Every explanation was met with another question. Family members still quote dearly departed Aunt Emma (pronounced Aint Emmer) who lost her temper with him when he was five. Somewhere exceeding a dozen questions, she blurted out, "There ain't no why to it!" But, that's just it. Some of us don't think like Aint Emmer. For us, part of wonder is wondering why.

I think we humans are loaded with questions starting with why because *homo sapiens* (Latin *sapiens* meaning *intelligence*[7]) were created in God's image. We were created with an impressively vast but finite capacity for understanding by a Creator with complete and infinite understanding. We want to know why because we want to understand. We want to understand because we were created in His image. One of countless things to deeply appreciate about God is that, while He steadfastly maintains the right to conceal certain explanations, He doesn't forbid us the right to ask why. The word *why* pops up 483 times in the CSB. Often He, who knows all answers, is the One asking. A smattering:

Jeremiah 44:7 "Why are you doing such terrible harm to yourselves?"

Matthew 9:4 "Why are you thinking evil things in your hearts?"

Matthew 26:10 "Why are you bothering this woman?"

Luke 24:38 "Why are you troubled?"

John 20:15 "Why are you crying?"

Choose two of the five, look up the context, and record it in this space.

Twenty-two times the psalmists ask the question *why*, including questions directed straight to God like "Why have you forgotten me?" (Ps. 42:9) and an astonishing "Wake up, LORD! Why are you sleeping?" (Ps. 44:23). God had not forgotten them nor does He sleep. However, His hands fashioned human emotions with an outlet: the mouth. When questions are brought to Him with sincere angst and pain, in pursuit of God-given understanding, crying out for the repair of intimacy's breach, He does not deny them volume. He may counter with questions of His own as in Job's case but not as a beating for asking. Hebrews 4:15 assures us that Jesus, our great high priest, is able to sympathize with us in every way. Surely this is one of the reasons the Holy Spirit preserved for us in permanent ink Christ's loud cry from the cross.

"Elí, Elí, lemá sabachtháni?" that is, "My God, my God, why have you forsaken me?"

MATTHEW 27:46, ESV

I appreciate the English language supplying a word that rolls from the depths of the soul and out of our mouths like a wail. If I may be so bold, *why* has the perfect phonetic to come forth like a primal howl. In our deepest pain when our souls feel like they're rupturing, we can throw our heads back, open our mouths wide and belt out, *Why?* We may often not get answers, but not because there ain't no why to it. Oh, yes, there is. It's just not time to hear it.

Remember the opening of our quest when we corresponded the five recalibrating questions to five of six oft-repeated investigative questions: *Who? What? Where? Why? How?* One investigative question was missing in our recalibrations and I assured you it would emerge at the end.

Which was missing?

For people of faith who take God at His word, many "ifs" get shoveled away, but there in the deep cleft echoes the question, *When?*

Lord, when?

I know You will ________________________ because You cannot lie, but when?

I know all things will work together for good, but when?

I know sowing seeds of Your Word reaps a harvest, but when?

I know You will defend Your own, but when?

I know joy comes in the morning, but when on earth will it be morning?

So often the testing is not so much in the believing but in the waiting. What are a few of your own current questions beginning with the words *Lord, when?*

On numerous occasions the psalmist cried, "How long, O Lord?" Here are two:

Lord, how long will you look on? Rescue me from their ravages; rescue my precious life.

PSALM 35:17

How long will the wicked celebrate?

PSALM 94:3

Revelation 6:9-11 poignantly depicts souls of martyrs under the altar crying out with a loud voice, "Lord, the one who is holy and true, how long until you judge those who live on the earth and avenge our blood? So they were each given a white robe, and they were told to rest a little while longer ..."

Read the following segments and explain how each one revolves around the question *When?*

Acts 1:6-8

1 Corinthians 13:9-12

1 Peter 5:4

1 John 2:28

To me, no segment of Scripture speaks more magnificently to when than 1 Peter 1:3-7. Read these verses from the NIV and circle three time frames: now/for a little while/when.

"Praise be to the God and Father of our Lord Jesus Christ! In his great mercy he has given us new birth into a living hope through the resurrection of Jesus Christ from the dead, and into an inheritance that can never perish, spoil or fade. This inheritance is kept in heaven for you, who through faith are shielded by God's power until the coming of the salvation that is ready to be revealed in the last time. In all this you greatly rejoice, though now for a little while you may have had to suffer grief in all kinds of trials. These have come so that the proven genuineness of your faith—of greater worth than gold, which perishes even though refined by fire—may result in praise, glory and honor when Jesus Christ is revealed."

As you run the course of your quest, know that in between your "now" and "when" is just "a little while." What seems long now will seem a heartbeat then. Let five words become the banner-waving answer to all that is ultimately worth waiting for: When Jesus Christ is revealed.

In the first advent, God wrapped His Son—the *Logos*, meaning Word—in swaddling clothes of flesh to dwell among mortals, and though Isaiah 53:2 informs us He had no beauty that they should desire Him, remarkably they did. Awakened by His Spirit, they were undistracted by His ordinariness and they beheld His glory, the glory of the One and Only (John 1:14). In the second advent all will behold the beauty of His holiness. Many will grieve that they did not believe, but all will gasp and bow at the excruciating sight of pure majesty.

Here we are, between those two advents. This One, who is our all, present among us, His Spirit within us, is hidden from our natural eyes. For now, quavering on the tight rope of faith suspended between those two visible appearings, the height of divine revelation is catching any glimpse of Christ's beauty. In all my years of life beating the life out of me, I have always and only come back to life one way: God dazzling me with Jesus.

May the unseen One, who fills all in all, peel away the cataracts our distractions have left on our spiritual eyes and grant us glimpses of Himself and the grace to bear and share them rightly. The whole earth is full of His glory, so keep your eyes wide open, Traveler. You are no aimless wanderer. Stay in the Scriptures. Seek the filling and thrilling of the Spirit. Savor good company. Sing, muse, dance, rest, and leap often. Laugh hard because life is hard and laughter is fine medicine. Don't keep your tears bottled up. Let them go, trusting God to be your bottler. That way none will go to waste.

You keep track of all my sorrows. You have collected all my tears in your bottle. You have recorded each one in your book.

PSALM 56:8, NLT

Anyway, blinking tears while reading Scripture can be like wipers on a filthy windshield. Suddenly you can see.

I could nod my head until my neck wrenched over these words from the pen of Oliver Wendell Holmes, Sr., "I wouldn't give a fig for the simplicity on the near side of complexity, but I would give my right arm for the simplicity on the far side of complexity."[8]

Those of us with quest in our blood will hunt the Word and world for thousands of scattered puzzle pieces. We'll shout praise to God for every discovery and exult over each handful of pieces that fit together. Still, no matter how long we live, we'll depart this place with hundreds of pieces strewn about. Then, finally, in eternity, we will open our eyes to every puzzle put together with seamless perfection comprising one solitary portrait. We will see His face and His name will be on our foreheads (Rev. 22:4).

I've always loved fireworks. I don't mind them loud. I like the way they burst the sky with fountains of light and how you can only really see them when it's dark outside. Boy, is it dark outside. How about you and I stand right here together for one final moment of our convergent quests and allow God to set off the densest set of questions in the New Testament like fireworks for a few adventurers who have come to appreciate them?

What then shall we say to these things? If God is for us, who can be against us? He who did not spare his own Son but gave him up for us all, how will he not also with him graciously give us all things? Who shall bring any charge against God's elect? It is God who justifies. Who is to condemn? Christ Jesus is the one who died—more than that, who was raised—who is at the right hand of God, who indeed is interceding for us. Who shall separate us from the love of Christ? Shall tribulation, or distress, or persecution, or famine, or nakedness, or danger, or sword?

ROMANS 8:31-35

Nope.

In all these things we are more than conquerors through him who loved us.

ROMANS 8:37

Stay the quest, Beloved of God. It's this, then bliss.

Return to Matthew 8:26 and allow the fourth recalibrating question to circle back around. Write it here.

The goal of the quest of faith is not to be fearless. It's to know you are never, ever Christ-less. Bring Him those fears. If you still have the same ones you recorded in Week One, talk to Him and ask Him to help you comprehend why they refuse to be quieted. If you have new ones, tell them to Him.

Record Christ's words in Matthew 14:27.

Note Christ's exhortation "Take courage!" (NIV). For your most stubborn fears, picture the process as an exchange. Hand Jesus your fears, and let Him trade you His courage.

Pen the words of Christ in Luke 12:32.

Who told you that?

Take a moment and reflect on your quest so far. Look back over each day of study and journal a brief note about what spoke to you, what you learned, and what course corrections you need to make. Then, spend a moment in prayer, writing from your heart to the Lord as you move forward on this quest.

DAY 1

Truths I encountered:

What I learned about myself and Jesus:

Course corrections I need to make:

DAY 2

Truths I encountered:

What I learned about myself and Jesus:

Course corrections I need to make:

DAY 3

Truths I encountered:

What I learned about myself and Jesus:

Course corrections I need to make:

DAY 4

Truths I encountered:

What I learned about myself and Jesus:

Course corrections I need to make:

DAY 5

Truths I encountered:

What I learned about myself and Jesus:

Course corrections I need to make:

Lord, as I move forward ...

Six

Farewell cheers for the quest ahead:

1. Read Psalm 119:17-19,89-105. __________ _____ _____ ________ ________.

2. Read Matthew 25:1-13. Keep the ________ in _____ __________.

3. Keep the __________ ________________.

4. Try not to ________ ____________ with _________ __________.

5. ___________ ______ _______________ when you _____. ___________ ___ when ________ _________.

6. Keep your ________ _______ _______ for _______________ works, _________, and _____________.

Video and audio sessions available for purchase at LifeWay.com/TheQuest.

#QuestStudy

LEADER GUIDE

What joy is in front of you as you lead your group through *The Quest*. Here are some things you need to know to be an effective leader.

FORMAT

The Quest is not your typical Beth Moore Bible study. How is it different?

No weekly theme

While some days of the week may loosely tie together, there is not an overarching theme. That is one reason there is no title for each week. Each day is a stop on this quest to intimacy with God.

Video format

While a regular Beth Moore Bible study has one-hour teaching for each session, *The Quest* only has two of those—the first session and the last. In between, each session video is approximately fifteen to twenty minutes. Those will include some question and answer time with Beth and Lauren Chandler, followed by a brief challenge for the week from Beth.

There are two options for meeting. You can meet every week to discuss and watch the video. You may also consider meeting on the first and sixth week to watch the longer videos together, while completing weeks two through five individually. Participants can download or rent those video sessions at LifeWay.com/TheQuest.

Daily studies

COMPASS – This part of the day's study lays the groundwork for your personal time with God. It looks a lot like what you would see in a regular Bible study from Beth—Scripture reading, commentary and illustrations, information and application questions.

QUERY – The second part of the study is designed to be a personal, focused time with God. Participants will be prompted through brief directives to answer questions and journal about a variety of things. What you journal is conversation between you and God. There will be space for journaling, but we would also encourage group members to get a blank journal to record notes and thoughts.

Assess Your Quest pages

When you're on a quest, it's good to periodically stop, take a moment, and take stock of the journey so far. At the end of each week, participants will get the opportunity to do that on this designated page. There is space provided for them to write what they learned, what course corrections they need to make, and their thoughts about moving forward. Group members have the option to assess immediately as they finish each day's lesson or wait until the end of the week to evaluate each day.

GROUP SESSIONS

This part of the study also looks a little different. Here are the elements for each group time:

Open

In the first session, you open with an icebreaker. In the following sessions, you will open with a review of the previous week's personal study. To begin discussion, encourage the participants to draw from their Assess Your Quest page for each week. To help prompt further response, feel free to use some or all of the questions listed in this section.

Watch

Watch the video for the session together. Keep in mind that Week One and Week Six videos are approximately one hour each. The other four are around fifteen to twenty minutes each.

Discuss

This will be the opportunity for your group to talk about what they learned and how they were impacted by the video teaching. There are several questions provided for you to stir the discussion.

Share

A quest seems to always go better when you have companions to join you. While each person must travel their own personal journey, it's vitally important that you have a group of fellow travelers encouraging you and holding you accountable. Take this time each week to move your group into small teams (three to four in a team). You have options on how the teams are formed.

OPTION 1 – If participants pre-registered, you can designate the makeup of each team.

OPTION 2 – You can allow teams to form themselves during this first session. Just make sure no one is left out and keep an eye on the dynamics of each team. You may need to step in and make some adjustments.

OPTION 3 – You may choose to wait until Session 2 to start the Share time. This will give you the opportunity to designate the teams after meeting each participant.

During the Share time, encourage participants to discuss honestly about where they are on the quest toward intimacy with God, hold each other accountable, and pray for one another. Inform them that they will meet together each week as a part of the group time.

Close

You will be given reminders and words of encouragement to share with your group, and/or prayer prompts to close your session.

Follow up

We understand that the lesson doesn't end with the final "Amen" on group meeting day. We urge you to pray for your group each week and to find ways to encourage and challenge them. We will provide brief ideas to help stir your creativity.

SESSION 1

Welcome participants. Begin compiling a group list where members can record their names, phone numbers, and email addresses.

OPEN

As an icebreaker, lead group members to share about their favorite trip. It could be a recent excursion or one from their youth or childhood. As they share, ask what made the trip special. Why was it memorable? After several have shared, ask: Would you call your favorite trip *a quest*? Why or why not?

Distribute *The Quest* books and encourage participants to follow the Session 1 viewer guide on page 10.

WATCH

View the Session 1 video (64:17).

DISCUSS

- What does the phrase "intimacy with God" mean to you? Would you say you have an intimate relationship with God? Why or why not? What does an intimate relationship with God look like?
- What's the difference between a quest and a trip? How is a quest more than just a trip?
- Why are questions essential for a trip to be a quest?
- What are some things that could be hindering your intimacy with God?

SHARE

Explain the purpose of this part of your group time. Move your group into small teams (three to four in a team).

CLOSE

Take a few minutes to point out the differences in this study from one of Beth's regular Bible studies. Encourage participants to move forward a few pages to preview the layout of each day's study. Point out the two different sections, especially noting the journaling recommended for each session.

Ask for questions. Close with prayer.

FOLLOW UP

Send an email or text to your group members telling them how glad and excited you are to launch into this quest alongside them.

SESSION 2

OPEN

Welcome participants and review what they learned in their personal study from last week. Encourage them to use their "Assess Your Quest" page (p. 42) to share truths they learned and course corrections they need to make. Also feel free to use the following questions to help prompt discussion.

- How do the recalibrating questions help you understand the current status of your relationship with Christ? Which recalibrating question was the most significant for you?
- Share about a time when you wondered why God was silent or if He had abandoned you.
- When you had to write five things you truly believe about yourself, did you find some things that couldn't be traced back to God? Explain.

- What are some desires God has planted deep in your heart? Have you seen those fulfilled? How are you dealing with the ones unfulfilled?
- How does the enemy use fear to stop you dead in your tracks?

WATCH

View the Session 2 video (20:10).

DISCUSS

Use the following questions to discuss the video:

- Ask a few of your group members to share how their quest with God started.
- Who are some people you know who have an intimate relationship with God? What characteristics mark their lives?
- Do you comprehend that you are filled with the Holy Spirit of God? How would it change your quest to truly know and believe that truth?
- Would you say that at this point on your quest with God, you are closer to being like the dry bones in the desert or fully alive in Him? Explain.

SHARE

Direct participants to move into their small groups to encourage, hold accountable, and pray for one another.

CLOSE

Encourage your group members to complete the five days of personal work before the next group session. Lead them in prayer, asking God to help you know and live the truth that the Holy Spirit lives in each follower of Christ.

FOLLOW UP

Send an email or text to your group members reminding them they are filled with God's Spirit.

SESSION 3

OPEN

Welcome participants and review what they learned in their personal study from last week. Encourage them to use their "Assess Your Quest" page (p. 82) to share truths they learned and course corrections they need to make. Also feel free to use the following questions to help prompt discussion.

- Do you ever get stuck in one place in your quest? What are you more likely to do, revel in the victories or wallow in the failures? Explain.
- Have you or are you currently experiencing a deep ache or longing over something you feel like God has not provided for you? Explain. How can you move forward from this?
- Share a time when God totally surprised you with what He did, when He did more than you could ask or imagine.
- Who is someone dear to your heart that you are interceding for? What is their need and how can we join you in praying for this person?
- On page 79, Beth encouraged you to make a bold request of God. Did you make one? If so, what was it?

WATCH

View the Session 3 video (14:19).

DISCUSS

Use the following questions to discuss the video:

- What is the difference in asking God questions and questioning God?
- Share a time that you found yourself asking God, "Lord, how could you let this happen?" How did God respond to you?
- When have you seen God do something in you, through you, or around you that you could not do on your own?
- When facing situations, do you always figure God in, or do you try to do things on your own?
- What do you have in your hand? What do you have to give to God that He can multiply to accomplish His purpose?

SHARE

Direct participants to move into their small groups to encourage, hold accountable, and pray for one another.

CLOSE

Challenge participants to daily allow God to use all they are for His glory. Remind them that He has gifted and equipped them to carry out His purpose and plan. Close in prayer.

FOLLOW UP

Send email or text this week with these words: "What is it you have in your hands?"

SESSION 4

OPEN

Welcome participants and review what they learned in their personal study from last week. Encourage them to use their "Assess Your Quest" page (p. 122) to share truths they learned and course corrections they need to make. Also feel free to use the following questions to help prompt discussion.

- In your quest toward intimacy with God, do you find yourself more often walking with purpose or wandering? Explain.
- Allow some participants to briefly share their conversion experiences.
- How does being a part of the kingdom of God factor into your daily living?
- How has the strength of God carried you and encouraged you in difficult times?
- How are you currently battling the enemy, and how can we pray for you?

WATCH

View Session 4 video (20:07).

DISCUSS

Use the following questions to discuss the video:

- Have you brought questions to Jesus that He has not answered yet? How do you continue to trust Him and keep moving forward?
- When was a time you just stood back in confusion or in wonder and asked "Who are you, Lord?"
- Has there been a time when you felt like no one really saw you, that you were invisible, that no one understood the real you? Explain.
- How has God made it known to you that He sees you?
- Have you ever been so self-aware that you missed what God was saying or

doing? Explain. How can you become more God-aware?

SHARE
Direct participants to move into their small groups to encourage, hold accountable, and pray for one another.

CLOSE
Remind group members that no matter what they face this week, God sees them, knows them, and is with them. Pray over your group that they would live in this truth this week.

FOLLOW UP
Send an email or text this week challenging your group members to be more God-aware in every situation of their lives.

SESSION 5

OPEN
Welcome participants and review what they learned in their personal study from last week. Encourage them to use their "Assess Your Quest" page (p. 164) to share truths they learned and course corrections they need to make. Also feel free to use the following questions to help prompt discussion.

- Share a time that you wrestled with God over a decision, situation, or circumstance.
- What are some significant markers in your life of faith—people, places, or events where you know God met you in a special, life-changing way?
- When have you walked through a time of suffering that was perhaps so deep that you questioned God's presence or His goodness? How was God faithful to you even in those moments?
- How have you helped others walk through a time of suffering?
- How has God fitted you for work in His kingdom? What gifts, talents, skills, etc., has He blessed you with, and how are you using them to serve Him?

WATCH
View Session 5 video (16:28).

DISCUSS
Use the following questions to discuss the video:

- How does the enemy use fear to interrupt your quest toward intimacy with God?
- What fear are you currently battling?
- What are your biggest distractions in your walk with the Lord?
- What other obstacles do you face in your life of faith?
- Why is it so important to put on the armor of God every day? Are you currently doing that? Explain.

SHARE
Direct participants to move into their small groups to encourage, hold accountable, and pray for one another.

CLOSE
Talk about how some distractions we'll face this week will be spontaneous situations and circumstances. However, most of us know already the things that will take our focus off of the quest. Lead the group to spend a few minutes in silence, laying those distractions before the Lord, and asking for His courage

and strength to not let those things get in the way of our relationships with Him this week. Call on two or three group members to close your time in prayer.

FOLLOW UP

Send an email or text this week with this message: "After you read this, if possible, set aside your technology for several hours and spend uninterrupted time with the Lord and your loved ones. If you're not able to do this immediately, designate several hours later in the day or evening to make this happen."

SESSION 6

OPEN

Welcome participants and review what they learned in their personal study from last week. Encourage them to use their "Assess Your Quest" page (p. 206) to share truths they learned and course corrections they need to make. Also feel free to use the following questions to help prompt discussion.

- What are some of the treasures of your faith walk you hold dear? Why?
- What are some of the ways your life has changed since the beginning of this quest?
- How have you seen the life of Christ grow in you after you went through a time of death working in you?
- How have you wasted time in your spiritual life because you were focused on competition or comparison?
- How is the way you're dealing with fear today different than it was in Week One?

WATCH

View Session 6 video (57:13).

DISCUSS

Use the following questions to discuss the video:

- Have you ever experienced a sense of delay between what is currently happening in your life and what God is calling you to? Explain.
- Share a time when you knew the Spirit of God was speaking to you through His Word.
- Is there anything in your life that is just dead weight to your walk of faith? It could be a relationship, a commitment, a habit, a hobby, etc. What is it that drags you down and holds you back in your quest for intimacy with God? What will it take to be shed of it?
- As you continue on this quest, are your eyes wide open to wondrous works, quirks, and perks? Why or why not? How can you maintain this attitude in your walk with the Lord?
- As you think back on this study ...
    - What is the most significant truth you encountered?
    - What is the biggest change you have made in your relationship with Christ?
    - How will your life and walk with the Lord be different because of what you've experienced?

SHARE

Direct participants to move into their small groups to encourage, hold accountable, and pray for one another.

CLOSE

Remind participants that the quest to intimacy with God isn't over with the end of this study. Point out the Questions for Your Quest on the following pages as tools for future study as participants continue in their quests. Challenge them to use what they've learned to springboard into a lifetime journey with God.

FOLLOW UP

In the space below, list several ways you can continue to encourage and challenge the group members in the coming weeks to persevere in their walk with the Lord.

Go to LifeWay.com/TheQuest for downloadable social media images to share what you're learning from this study with your friends.

Endnotes

VIEWER GUIDE ONE

1. *Merriam-Webster's Collegiate Dictionary*, 11th ed. (Springfield, MA: Merriam-Webster, Inc., 2003)
2. Ibid.

SESSION ONE

1. J. L. Hancock, *All the Questions in the Bible*, (Oak Harbor, WA: Logos Research Systems, Inc., 1998), iii.
2. C. Brand, C. Draper, A. England, S. Bond, E. R., Clendenen, and T. C. Butler, eds. "Jeshurun," *Holman Illustrated Bible Dictionary* (Nashville, TN: Holman Bible Publishers, 2003), 899.
3. Angela Duckworth, *Grit* (New York, NY: Scribner, 2016), 247-248.
4. "What A Friend We Have In Jesus," Joseph M. Scriven, 1855.
5. William Temple, *Readings in St. John's Gospel* (London, UK: MacMillan and Company Limited, 1963), 29.
6. D. A. Hagner, *Matthew 1–13*, vol. 33A, Word Biblical Commentary, eds. David A. Hubbard and Glenn W. Barker (Grand Rapids, MI: Zondervan, 2000), 220.
7. T. R. McNeal, "Luke," *Holman Illustrated Bible Dictionary*, eds. C. Brand, C. Draper, A. England, S. Bond, E. R. Clendenen, and T. C. Butler (Nashville, TN: Holman Bible Publishers, 2003), 1057.
8. Ibid.

SESSION TWO

1. K. A. Mathews, *Genesis 11:27–50:26*, vol. 1B, The New American Commentary (Nashville: Broadman & Holman Publishers, 2005), 172.
2. W. M. Alston, Jr., as quoted by V. P. Hamilton, *The Book of Genesis, Chapters 18–50* (Grand Rapids, MI: Wm. B. Eerdmans Publishing Co, 1995), 8.
3. Ibid., 11.
4. Ibid., 9.
5. G. J. Wenham, *Genesis 16–50*, Vol. 2, Word Biblical Commentary, eds. David A. Hubbard and Glenn W. Barker (Grand Rapids, MI: Zondervan, 2000), 47.
6. Hamilton, 17.
7. Mathews, 226.
8. N. T. Wright, *John for Everyone* (London, UK: Society for Promoting Christan Knowledge, 2004), 8.
9. C. S. Lewis, *Till We Have Faces* (Orlando, FL: Harcourt, 1956), 75-76.

SESSION THREE

1. J. Newell, " Zion," *Holman Illustrated Bible Dictionary*, eds. C. Brand, C. Draper, A. England, S. Bond, E. R. Clendenen, and T. C. Butler (Nashville, TN: Holman Bible Publishers, 2003) , 1711–1712.
2. *Merriam-Webster's Collegiate Dictionary*, 11th ed. (Springfield, MA: Merriam-Webster, Inc., 2003), 1408.
3. Ibid.
4. Russell Moore, *Onward* Bible Study (Nashville, TN: LifeWay Press, 2005), 21.
5. Alexander Schmemann, *For The Life Of The World* (Crestwood, NY: St. Vladimir's Seminary Press, 2004), 29.
6. "The Wizard of Oz: An American Fairy Tale," Library of Congress, accessed July 3, 2017, http://www.loc.gov/exhibits/oz/ozsect2.html.
7. S. Zodhiates, *The Complete Word Study Dictionary: New Testament*, (Chattanooga, TN: AMG Publishers, 1993) accessed on July 3, 2017 via mywsb.com, 736.
8. Ibid., 639.
9. *Merriam-Webster's Collegiate Dictionary*, 43.
10. J. B. Green, *The Gospel of Luke* (Grand Rapids, MI: Wm. B. Eerdmans Publishing Co., 1997), 419.
11. Zodhiates, 63.
12. Zodhiates, 418.

SESSION FOUR

1. Genesis 32:28 Footnote, *Christian Standard Bible* (Nashville, TN: Holman Bible Publishers, 2017), 28.
2. Hamilton, 329.
3. Rabbi Ted Falcon and David Blatner, *Judaism for Dummies* (Hoboken, NJ: John Wiley and Sons, Inc., 2013), 24.
4. Ibid, 322.
5. Hancock, iii.
6. H. Hunt, "Job, Book Of," *Holman Illustrated Bible Dictionary*, eds. C. Brand, C. Draper, A. England, S. Bond, E. R. Clendenen, and T. C. Butler (Nashville, TN: Holman Bible Publishers, 2003), 924.
7. R. L. Alden, *The New American Commentary: Volume 11, Job* (Nashville: Broadman & Holman Publishers, 1993).
8. John Piper, "When Words Are Wind" *Desiring God* November 10, 1993, accessed on July 3, 2017, available online via desiringgod.org/articles/when-words-are-wind.
9. J. E. Hartley, *The New International Commentary on the Old Testament: The Book of Job* (Grand Rapids, MI: Wm. B. Eerdmans Publishing Co., 1988), accessed on July 3, 2017 via mywsb.com.
10. Ibid., 490.
11. R.B. Dillard, *World Biblical Commentary: 2 Chronicles* (Dallas: Word Books, 1987), 71.
12. Ibid.
13. Frank E. Gaebelein (Ed.), *The Expositor's Bible Commentary: 1 & 2 Kings, 1 & 2 Chronicles, Ezra, Nehemiah, Esther, Job*, Volume 4 (Grand Rapids: Zondervan, 1988) accessed on July 3, 2017 via mywsb.com.

SESSION FIVE

1. Zodhiates, 225
2. R. T. France, *The Gospel of Matthew* (Grand Rapids: Wm. B. Eerdmans Publication Co., 2007), 546-547.
3. Zodhiates, 1150.
4. Saint Augustine, R. S. Pine-Coffin, *Confessions* (London: Penguin Books, 1961).
5. Zodhiates, 1180.
6. Hancock, iii.
7. "Definition of Homo Sapiens," *Merriam-Webster's Dictionary*. Accessed on July 3, 2017, Available online via merriam-webster.com/dictionary/Homo%20sapiens.
8. Oliver Wendell Holmes, Sr. as quoted in Stephen R. Covey, *The 8th Habit: From Effectiveness to Greatness* (New York: Free Press, 2004), 103.

QUESTIONS FOR YOUR QUEST

Listed below are several additional questions from Scripture you can use for personal study in your continued quest toward intimacy with God. We included the immediate context of each passage in parentheses.

WHO?

But Moses asked God, "Who am I that I should go to Pharaoh and that I should bring the Israelites out of Egypt?"

EXODUS 3:11 (EXODUS 3:1–4:17)

Then I heard the voice of the Lord asking: Who should I send? Who will go for us? I said: Here I am. Send me.

ISAIAH 6:8 (ISAIAH 6:1-8)

When Jesus came to the region of Caesarea Philippi, he asked his disciples, "Who do people say that the Son of Man is?"

MATTHEW 16:13 (MATTHEW 16:13-20)

"But you," he asked them, "who do you say that I am?"

MATTHEW 16:15 (MATTHEW 16:13-20)

At that time the disciples came to Jesus and said, "So who is greatest in the kingdom of heaven?"

MATTHEW 18:1 (MATTHEW 18:1-9)

But wanting to justify himself, he asked Jesus, "And who is my neighbor?"

LUKE 10:29 (LUKE 10:25-37)

So if you have not been faithful with worldly wealth, who will trust you with what is genuine? And if you have not been faithful with what belongs to someone else, who will give you what is your own?

LUKE 16:11-12 (LUKE 16:1-13)

For who is greater, the one at the table or the one serving? Isn't it the one at the table? But I am among you as the one who serves.

LUKE 22:27 (LUKE 22:24-30)

"Who is he, Sir, that I may believe in him?" he asked.

JOHN 9:36 (JOHN 9:1-41)

"Who are you, Lord?" Saul said. "I am Jesus, the one you are persecuting," he replied.

ACTS 9:5 (ACTS 9:1-18)

WHAT?

But Abram said, "Lord GOD, what can you give me, since I am childless and the heir of my house is Eliezer of Damascus?"

GENESIS 15:2 (GENESIS 15:1-21)

What is a human being that you remember him, a son of man that you look after him?

PSALM 8:4 (PSALM 8:1-9)

Jesus stopped, called them, and said, "What do you want me to do for you?"

MATTHEW 20:32 (MATTHEW 20:29-34)

If you love those who love you, what credit is that to you? Even sinners love those who love them.

LUKE 6:32 (LUKE 6:27-36)

To what then should I compare the people of this generation, and what are they like?

LUKE 7:31 (LUKE 7:31-35)

For what does it benefit someone if he gains the whole world, and yet loses or forfeits himself?

LUKE 9:25 (LUKE 9:23-27)

A ruler asked him, "Good teacher, what must I do to inherit eternal life?"

LUKE 18:18 (LUKE 18:18-23)

"What does that have to do with you and me, woman?" Jesus asked. "My hour has not yet come."

JOHN 2:4 (JOHN 2:1-12)

"What is truth?" said Pilate.

JOHN 18:38 (JOHN 18:28-40)

What should we say then? Should we continue in sin so that grace may multiply?

ROMANS 6:1 (ROMANS 6:1-14)

WHEN? (ALSO HOW LONG?)

Then Elijah approached all the people and said, "How long will you waver between two opinions? If the Lord is God, follow him. But if Baal, follow him." But the people didn't answer him a word.

1 KINGS 18:21 (1 KINGS 18:20-40)

How long, LORD? Will you forget me forever? How long will you hide your face from me?

PSALM 13:1 (PSALM 13:1-6)

I thirst for God, the living God. When can I come and appear before God?

PSALM 42:2 (PSALM 42:1-11)

Then the righteous will answer him, "Lord, when did we see you hungry and feed you, or thirsty and give you something to drink? When did we see you a stranger and take you in, or without clothes and clothe you? When did we see you sick, or in prison, and visit you?"

MATTHEW 25:37-39 (MATTHEW 25:31-46)

Tell us, when will these things happen? And what will be the sign when all these things are about to be accomplished?

MARK 13:4 (MARK 13:1-37)

I tell you that he will swiftly grant them justice. Nevertheless, when the Son of Man comes, will he find faith on earth?

LUKE 18:8 (LUKE 18:1-8)

He also said to them, "When I sent you out without money-bag, traveling bag, or sandals, did you lack anything?"

LUKE 22:35 (LUKE 22:35-38)

When they found him on the other side of the sea, they said to him, "Rabbi, when did you get here?"

JOHN 6:25 (JOHN 6:1-70)

However, many from the crowd believed in him and said, "When the Messiah comes, he won't perform more signs than this man has done, will he?"

JOHN 7:31 (JOHN 7:25-36)

The Jews surrounded him and asked, "How long are you going to keep us in suspense? If you are the Messiah, tell us plainly."

JOHN 10:24 (JOHN 10:22-30)

WHERE?

Where can I go to escape your Spirit? Where can I flee from your presence?

PSALM 139:7 (PSALM 139:1-16)

On the first day of Unleavened Bread the disciples came to Jesus and asked, "Where do you want us to make preparations for you to eat the Passover?"

MATTHEW 26:17 (MATTHEW 26:17-30)

His disciples answered him, "Where can anyone get enough bread here in this desolate place to feed these people?"

MARK 8:4 (MARK 8:1-10)

He said to them, "Where is your faith?" They were fearful and amazed, asking one another, "Who then is this? He commands even the winds and the waves, and they obey him!"

LUKE 8:25 (LUKE 8:22-25)

"Sir," said the woman, "you don't even have a bucket, and the well is deep. So where do you get this 'living water'?"

JOHN 4:11 (JOHN 4:1-42)

When Jesus stood up, he said to her, "Woman, where are they? Has no one condemned you?"

JOHN 8:10 (JOHN 8:2-11)

"Where have you put him?" he asked. "Lord," they told him, "come and see."

JOHN 11:34 (JOHN 11:1-44)

"Lord," Simon Peter said to him, "where are you going?" Jesus answered, "Where I am going you cannot follow me now, but you will follow later."

JOHN 13:36 (JOHN 13:36-38)

If the whole body were an eye, where would the hearing be? If the whole body were an ear, where would the sense of smell be?

1 CORINTHIANS 12:17 (1 CORINTHIANS 12:1-31)

Where, death, is your victory? Where, death, is your sting?

1 CORINTHIANS 15:55 (1 CORINTHIANS 15:50-58)

WHY?

Why, my soul, are you so dejected? Why are you in such turmoil? Put your hope in God, for I will still praise him, my Savior and my God.

PSALM 42:11 (PSALM 42:1-11)

Why do you look at the splinter in your brother's eye but don't notice the beam of wood in your own eye?

MATTHEW 7:3 (MATTHEW 7:1-6)

Then the disciples came up and asked him, "Why are you speaking to them in parables?"

MATTHEW 13:10 (MATTHEW 13:1-23)

Sighing deeply in his spirit, he said, "Why does this generation demand a sign? Truly I tell you, no sign will be given to this generation."

MARK 8:12 (MARK 8:11-21)

"Why do you call me good?" Jesus asked him. "No one is good except God alone."

MARK 10:18 (MARK 10:17-22)

"Why were you searching for me?" he asked them. "Didn't you know that it was necessary for me to be in my Father's house?"

LUKE 2:49 (LUKE 2:41-50)

But perceiving their thoughts, Jesus replied to them, "Why are you thinking this in your hearts?"

LUKE 5:22 (LUKE 5:17-26)

Why do you call me "Lord, Lord," and don't do the things I say?

LUKE 6:46 (LUKE 6:46-49)

"Why are you troubled?" he asked them. "And why do doubts arise in your hearts?"

LUKE 24:38 (LUKE 24:36-49)

Falling to the ground, he heard a voice saying to him, "Saul, Saul, why are you persecuting me?"

ACTS 9:4 (ACTS 9:1-18)

HOW?

How can a young man keep his way pure? By keeping your word.

PSALM 119:9 (PSALM 119:9-16)

You have turned things around, as if the potter were the same as the clay. How can what is made say about its maker, "He didn't make me"? How can what is formed say about the one who formed it, "He doesn't understand what he's doing"?

ISAIAH 29:16 (ISAIAH 29:1-24)

Then Peter approached him and asked "Lord, how many times shall I forgive my brother or sister who sins against me? As many as seven times?"

MATTHEW 18:21 (MATTHEW 18:21-35)

If that's how God clothes the grass, which is in the field today and is thrown into the furnace tomorrow, how much more will he do for you—you of little faith?

LUKE 12:28 (LUKE 12:22-34)

When he came to his senses, he said, "How many of my father's hired workers have more than enough food, and here I am dying of hunger!"

LUKE 15:17 (LUKE 15:11-32)

"Lord," Thomas said, "we don't know where you're going. How can we know the way?"

JOHN 14:5 (JOHN 14:1-7)

How, then, can they call on him they have not believed in? And how can they believe without hearing about him? And how can they hear without a preacher? And how can they preach unless they are sent? As it is written: How beautiful are the feet of those who bring good news.

ROMANS 10:14-15 (ROMANS 10:1-21)

Now if Christ is proclaimed as raised from the dead, how can some of you say, "There is no resurrection of the dead"?

1 CORINTHIANS 15:12
(1 CORINTHIANS 15:1-58)

How will we escape if we neglect such a great salvation? This salvation had its beginning when it was spoken of by the Lord, and it was confirmed to us by those who heard him.

HEBREWS 2:3 (HEBREWS 2:1-4)

Take the next step in your
Bible study experience.